Scarecrow Film Score Guides

Series Editor: Kate Daubney

CW00821116

The Good, the Bad and the Ugly
© 1966 Alberto Grimaldi Productions S.A.
All Rights Reserved
Courtesy of MGM CLIP+STILL

Ennio Morricone's
The Good, the Bad and the Ugly

A Film Score Guide

Charles Leinberger

Scarecrow Film Score Guides, No. 3

The Scarecrow Press, Inc.
Lanham, Maryland • Toronto • Oxford
2004

SCARECROW PRESS, INC.

Published in the United States of America
by Scarecrow Press, Inc.
A wholly owned subsidiary of
The Rowman & Littlefield Publishing Group, Inc.
4501 Forbes Boulevard, Suite 200, Lanham, Maryland 20706
www.scarecrowpress.com

PO Box 317
Oxford
OX2 9RU, UK

British Library Cataloguing in Publication Information Available

Library of Congress Cataloging-in-Publication Data

Leinberger, Charles, 1955–
  Ennio Morricone's The good, the bad and the ugly : a film score guide /
Charles Leinberger.
     p. cm. — (Scarecrow film score guides ; no. 3)
  Includes bibliographical references and index.
  ISBN 0-8108-5132-6 (pbk. : alk. paper)
  1. Morricone, Ennio. Good, the bad and the ugly. I. Title. II. Series.
ML410.M79L45 2004
781.5'42–dc22   2004008692

To Andrea —
with whom I have had the pleasure of
sharing this journey called life,
and without whom many things would not be possible

CONTENTS

FIGURES

EDITOR'S FOREWORD

The Scarecrow series of Film Score Guides is a set of books dedicated to drawing together the variety of different analytical practices and ideological approaches in film musicology for the study of individual scores. Much value has been drawn from case studies of film scoring practice in other film music texts, but these guides offer a substantial, wide-ranging, and comprehensive study of a single score. Subjects are chosen for the series on the basis that they have become and are widely recognized as a benchmark for the way in which film music is composed and experienced. Each guide explores the context of a score's composition through its place in the career of the composer and its relationship to the techniques of the composer. The context of the score in narrative and production terms is also considered, and readings of the film as a whole are discussed in order to situate the musical analyses which conclude the guide in their filmic context. Furthermore, although these guides focus on the score as written text, bringing forward often previously unknown details about the process of composition as they are manifested in the manuscript, analysis also includes exploration of the music as an aural text, for this is the first and, for most audiences, the only way in which they will experience the music of the film.

This volume on *The Good, the Bad and the Ugly* has benefited from the willingness of Ennio Morricone to be interviewed by Dr. Leinberger, for which Scarecrow Press and I are extremely grateful. In film musicology, the input of the composer is particularly valuable, because while filmic experience is necessarily subjective to the audience, it is also subjective to the composer. Learning how a composer translates this to the compositional process enhances and expands the ways in which we may interpret and analyze film music, an advantage which will continue to stimulate scholars and filmgoers alike. As readers of this volume will discover, Signor Morricone's comments about his own work are incisive yet intuitive, highlighting a side of compositional process that is often hidden by a more clinical analytical agenda: that despite the collaborative context of working closely with a director, writing music is still an instinctive, creative process.

The Good, the Bad and the Ugly is a film which has marked the consciousness of many of those who have seen it, perhaps because its main title sequence provides one of the most recognizable motifs in all music. The score is an exercise in compact expression, and the opening phrases not only encapsulate but, arguably, now define the physical space of the film in a way that few scores for other films have ever achieved. This volume explores exactly how Morricone achieved this, using a range of models that will enable the reader, whatever his or her level of musical knowledge or understanding, to learn more about what part the music plays in this memorable film.

Dr. Kate Daubney
Series Editor

PREFACE

As a graduate student at the University of Arizona, I was required to have two minor fields of study in addition to my major field of music theory. Although I had no trouble choosing my music minor, trumpet performance, my nonmusic minor required some serious thought, but I finally decided to study media arts. It was as a student of media arts that I found myself taking a graduate research seminar, the topic of which was the films of Clint Eastwood.

During this seminar, we spent some time studying the Westerns of Sergio Leone, the Hollywood Westerns, the *Dirty Harry* films, the comedies, and others. It was in this class that I first saw *A Fistful of Dollars*. When I read "music by Dan Savio" in the opening credits, I thought to myself, "Dan Savio? No, this music can only be that of Ennio Morricone!" I soon learned that it was.

The seminar's professor, Dr. Peter Lehman, knew I was a student of music theory and wanted me to add a musical perspective to our critical discussion whenever possible. When he was choosing films for each student's research paper and class presentation, we both smiled when I suggested that I should do my project on *The Good, the Bad and the Ugly*, since we both knew that Ennio Morricone's music for that film was very innovative for its time. My unpublished research paper of December 1995, which was titled *Every Gun Makes Its Own Tune*, was my first serious look at the music of Ennio Morricone and the multifaceted score he created for this film.

I was fascinated by the uniqueness of this music and I was nothing less than mesmerized by the film itself. The climactic ending of the film and its equally climactic music represent a union of image and sound that is rarely achieved in any film genre. I enjoyed studying this film and its evocative score. The more I learned about the pioneering music of Ennio Morricone, the more I wanted to learn.

After this seminar, I went on to write my dissertation on Max Steiner's Academy-Award-winning music for the 1942 Bette Davis film *Now, Voyager*, a magnificent example of a classic Hollywood film score. But I had always hoped to return to the more eclectic music of Ennio Morricone someday because of its unique manipulation of musical colors and hues that many film composers often choose not to explore.

As a student listening to his film scores, I would often ask myself why this music sounds so unmistakably "Morriconian" and what in the music gives it this distinguishing character. Needless to say, I was delighted when Dr. Kate Daubney invited me to contribute to this series of film score guides for Scarecrow Press by more deeply exploring Morricone's compositional style. I was equally delighted when I contacted Maestro Morricone and he agreed to meet with me for an interview as part of my research for this guide.

In July of 2003 I had the pleasure of meeting Maestro Morricone at his home in Rome. During this meeting, he sat at the piano in his living room and played the A section of the "Main Title" from *The Good, the Bad and the Ugly*. It was one of those rare and unexpected moments when one is able to hear music performed by its composer. He is in person as expressive and energetic as his music. He articulates his ideas in conversation, in Italian naturally, as clearly as he does in his music. Through this guide, I hope to share some of the excitement and intensity of Ennio Morricone's music that I experienced that day.

ACKNOWLEDGMENTS

This book may be many things, but it most certainly is not a solo effort. There are many generous and supportive people without whom this project simply would not have been possible. I sincerely hope that this small expression of gratitude will begin to return the many favors that they have contributed.

First and foremost, I must express my sincere thanks to Maestro Ennio Morricone, who was kind enough to respond to all of my correspondences and found the time to meet with me for an interview, even though he remains a very busy composer, orchestrator, and conductor.

I would also like to thank Eli Wallach for taking time out of his busy schedule to allow me to conduct a telephone interview. His kindness, generosity, and sense of humor are greatly appreciated.

Although it was difficult at first to find someone in El Paso, Texas, who speaks Italian fluently, I could not have asked for anyone more knowledgeable and more helpful than Albert Balesh, M.D., who donated a great deal of time to translate correspondences to and from Maestro Morricone. Dr. Balesh was also kind to permit me to enroll in his Italian classes even though I never had enough time to study adequately.

I consider myself quite fortunate to know Sergio Miceli, Professor of History of Film Music at the University of Florence, Italy, who made it possible for me to correspond directly with Maestro Morricone. Professor Miceli's publications on Morricone's film music proved to be an essential part of my research for this guide. With his approval, many of the musical examples contained herein have been modeled after his work. His contribution to this guide is immeasurable.

I must thank Sister Mary Sarah Braun, S.N.D. (Sisters of Notre Dame), who, on very short notice, offered to be my interpreter when I met with Maestro Morricone, as well as my chauffeur and guide. Without her help I could not have found my way through Rome to meet with Maestro Morricone and conduct a successful interview.

Sincere thanks go to I.R.TE.M., Istituto di Ricerca per il Teatro Musicale, Rome, Italy, for introducing me to Professor Miceli and for making available their unique resources on Ennio Morricone.

As a result of Maestro Morricone's advice, I also found a colleague in Philip Tagg, Ph.D., Professor of Musicology at the University of Montréal. I further consider myself fortunate to have found colleagues in Robert C. Cumbow, J.D., Seattle University School of Law; Professor Sir Christopher Frayling, Rector and Vice-Provost, Royal College of Art (London); and Jeff Smith, Ph.D., Director of Film and Media Studies, Washington University in St. Louis.

Through my research on Max Steiner, I was fortunate to find a colleague and friend in Kate Daubney, Ph.D., Visiting Research Fellow in Film Music Studies at the University of Leeds and editor of this series.

I would also like to acknowledge Cynthia Farah Haines, Assistant Professor of Film Studies, the University of Texas at El Paso; Juliette Perez, Copyright Coordinator, Warner Bros. Publications, Inc.; Ivy Kwong, MGM Clip+Still Licensing; and Margarita Lopez-Urrutia and Marco Pennacchini, translators. Heartfelt thanks also go to the many fine staff members at the Scarecrow Press, Inc.

There are many other friends, colleagues, students, and family members who have given me moral support and guidance throughout this project and to whom I am indebted.

INTRODUCTION

The third of Sergio Leone's three Westerns starring Clint Eastwood, *The Good, the Bad and the Ugly*, like its two predecessors, *A Fistful of Dollars* and *For a Few Dollars More*, significantly altered the perception that moviegoers of the 1960s had of the old American West. The old West was no longer thought of as a time and a place where the good guys wore white hats and the bad guys wore black ones, as did James Cagney and Humphrey Bogart in *The Oklahoma Kid* (1939). It was now a world where the line that separated good and evil became blurred to the point where, in this film, director Sergio Leone chose to freeze the action and take the time to tell the audience on screen which protagonist was in fact "the good," which one was "the bad," and also, which one was "the ugly." It was a time and a place where the hero was almost as evil, selfish, greedy, and amoral as the villain he sought to destroy. In Leone's version of the old American West, all men had within them some good, some evil, and some ugliness.

It seems only fitting, therefore, that such a paradigm shift in the moral code of the Western be accompanied by an equally dramatic shift in the role played by the music of that genre. Assimilating many musical influences of the pop culture of the time, Ennio Morricone's music for *The Good, the Bad and the Ugly* gave audiences a new musical language whose vocabulary appeared to have little in common with its Hollywood predecessors. It is a musical language where the line separating music and sound effects also became blurred, where dynamics and tone color placed the music on a level equal to the film's dialogue and not subservient to it. It soon became a musical language imitated by others, including Hollywood film composers. Ennio Morricone's score for *The Good, the Bad and the Ugly* is nothing less than a milestone in the stylistic evolution of film music, not just for the Western genre, but for all of cinema.

This guide is intended to demonstrate Morricone's unique and enduring contributions to the art of film music through a discussion of his compositional and orchestrational processes, many of which are evident in his music for *The Good, the Bad and the Ugly*, in a way that can easily be understood by both musicians and nonmusicians. It begins with a brief discussion of his musical background, from his early musical influences through his musical education in Rome, his experiences in the Italian music business, his earliest Italian film scores, and his accomplishments in Hollywood. The second chapter discusses the many compositional techniques that distinguish Morricone's music from that of other film composers. There are many elements that make his compositional style easily recognizable, what he calls his own "calligraphy," and these elements will be explained in detail. The third chapter gives the reader a historical perspective in which to place Morricone's music for *The Good, the Bad and the Ugly*, as a means of understanding how this film and its music may have been perceived by American audiences in the 1960s. The fourth chapter places this particular film score stylistically among Morricone's other well-known scores, particularly those for Sergio Leone's other Westerns. Understanding the music's context will also help the reader understand many of the details discussed in the final chapter, which is an analysis of Morricone's themes for *The Good, the Bad and the Ugly* and the compositional techniques that he uses throughout the film, presented in chronological order, from the film's opening credits to its climactic ending.

Although this guide will focus on Morricone and his music from a theoretical, structural, and formal point of view, other nonmusical issues which are relevant to the audience's perception of the music as part of the viewing experience will also be discussed. Indeed, it is often difficult, if not impossible, to separate Morricone's music from other sonic and visual elements of this film.

1

ENNIO MORRICONE'S
MUSICAL BACKGROUND

Five-time Academy Award nominee Ennio Morricone, one of the most prolific, innovative, and recognizable film composers ever, was born into a musical family on 10 November 1928 in a residential area of Rome known as Trastevere, which is across the Tiber River from the heart of Rome. The oldest child of Mario Morricone and Libera Ridolfi, he began his musical life playing trumpet. As a composer, his fondness for that majestic instrument would be evident throughout his career by its presence in many of his best-known film score themes.

Education and Early Influences

Ennio Morricone demonstrated his exceptional musical ability and his flair for musical creativity at an early age. Jay Cocks, who interviewed Morricone for *Time* magazine in 1987, learned that "Morricone's father was a trumpet player who performed jazz and opera and worked on movie scores. His son started to write music . . . at the age of six."[1] Approximately two years later, when Ennio was about eight years old and attending John the Baptist Elementary School in Rome, he met Sergio Leone, with whom he would form a very fruitful artistic partnership many years later. Morricone's musical abilities continued to develop rapidly throughout his childhood. Cocks adds, "When he was twelve, his parents enrolled him in the Rome music conservatory, where he finished a four-year harmony course in six months."[2] The school was Santa Cecilia Conservatory where Morricone continued his trumpet studies with Umberto Semproni. While he was attending Santa Cecilia, one of his harmony teachers, Roberto Caggiano, suggested that he begin to study composition. Shortly thereafter, Morricone began studying composition with Carlo Garofalo and Antonio Ferdinandi and eventually concluded his composition studies at Santa Cecilia with Goffredo Petrassi.[3] Petrassi, himself a graduate of Santa Cecilia, was one of the major figures of twentieth-century Italian composition. He is best known for his seven concertos for orchestra, but he also wrote several film scores from the late 1940s through the early 1960s.

Before receiving his diplomas in trumpet, band instrumentation, and composition from the conservatory, Morricone had already begun composing background music for radio dramas.[4] He was also active as a trumpet player, often performing in an orchestra that specialized in music written for films. As he told Adam Sweeting of *The Guardian* in 2001, "Most of these scores were very ugly, and I believed I could do better than this. After the war, the film industry was quite strong here in Italy, and the New Realism in Italian cinema was really wonderful, but these new realistic movies didn't have great music. I needed money and I thought it would be a good thing to write film scores."[5] Some influences of the New Realism are evident in Leone's films where, compared to the so-called Hollywood invisible style, space and time are not as fragmented. For example, when somebody is seen walking down a hallway, a staircase, or a street, Leone often includes every step of that person's movement, rather than letting the audience assume that the person has made the complete trip. One example of this realistic style occurs early in *The Good, the Bad and the Ugly* (1966, released in the United States in 1967) as Angel Eyes (Lee Van Cleef) enters a farmhouse and slowly walks from the entrance to the dining room table. The audience sees every step he takes. It is this element of realism, lengthy shots that often include little dialogue, that gives Morricone's music the opportunity to be heard above all other sounds.

Inspiration and financial need would eventually lead Morricone to the compositions for which he is best known, film music. His film music scores, however, as will be seen, represent only a small portion of his total output as a composer. He continues to write very modern and experimental concert music as well.

Italy

Although he received what might be considered a classical music education, Morricone soon found himself working in the Italian popular music industry as a means of supporting himself and his family (he was married in 1956 and he and his wife had their first child the following year). After accepting a position with the Italian broadcasting company RAI in 1958 as a music assistant, a position he held for one day, he was soon working for RCA. Jeff Smith observes:

> After completing his education at Saint Cecilia, Morricone honed his orchestration skills as an arranger for Italian radio and television. In order to support himself, he moved to RCA in the early sixties and entered the front ranks of the Italian recording industry. As a top studio arranger, Morricone provided orchestrations for more than five hundred songs and worked with such recording artists as Mario Lanza, Paul Anka, and Chet Baker. During this period, Morricone developed a facility with a number of pop idioms, including rock, jazz, and Neapolitan love songs.[6]

No doubt it was Morricone's expertise in the popular music business and his familiarity with popular trends in Europe in particular, in addition to his proficiency as an orchestrator and conductor, that enabled him to create film scores that were not only successful as artistic components of the films, but were also commercially successful soundtrack recordings. The influences of the popular music of the 1960s, such as the use of the electric guitar, are evident in his score for *The Good, the Bad and the Ugly*, as well as his other film scores, both Westerns and non-Westerns.

The Westerns of Sergio Leone

Morricone began composing film music in 1961 with the score to *Il federale*, which was released in the United States in 1965. Laurence MacDonald explains some of the events leading up to this project:

> It was his work in the Italian theater that steered him in the direction of film. After working with director Luciano Salce on a number of plays, Morricone was hired by Salce to compose his first film score, the music for the 1961 film *Il federale*.[7]

In the years that followed, Morricone went on to compose music for many more Italian films, some of which were Westerns. Although this Italian-made subgenre of the Western is often referred to as the "spaghetti Western," a term first used by American film critics, Morricone finds such a label to be "both annoying and unpleasant."[8] In 1964, Morricone composed the music for Sergio Leone's first Western, *A Fistful of Dollars* (released in the United States in 1967), even though he appears in the opening credits as "Dan Savio." Likewise, Gian Maria Volonté (who played Ramón Rojo) appears as "Johnny Wels" in that film's credits and Sergio Leone appears as "Bob Robertson" in the credits of some European prints of that film. Leone biographer Christopher Frayling explains the strategy behind the use of less Italian-sounding pseudonyms: "So that *Italian* audiences would not think that *Fistful* was home-made, the distributors made most of the cast and crew hide behind pseudonyms."[9] This deception apparently worked, and Italian audiences, who had demonstrated a declining interest in home-made Westerns, turned out in large numbers to see Leone's contributions to that genre. When the next Leone Western, *Per qualche dollaro in più (For a Few Dollars More)*, was released in Italy in 1965, Leone and Morricone apparently no longer had any need for such pseudonyms.

Although Leone and Morricone were schoolmates in the 1930s, the two men apparently had not maintained a friendship after childhood. They were reacquainted in the 1960s through their work on Westerns. Christopher Frayling explains the circumstances surrounding their reunion and the subsequent scoring of Leone's films:

When Morricone was approached to write the music for *Fistful*, he was working on Caiano's *Pistols Don't Argue*. The *Pistols* soundtrack is not particularly interesting: a fully orchestrated main theme, based on a four-chord structure, with a French horn taking the tune, backed by insistent "hoofbeat" drums—all reminiscent of the Hollywood equivalent. *Pistols Don't Argue* even has a traditional ballad entitled "Lonesome Billy," sung by Peter Tevis. Sergio Leone thought Morricone's early film scores terrible—and Morricone . . . apparently agreed. But Morricone had produced (anonymously) a strange arrangement of the American folk-song "Pastures of Plenty": Leone found this more interesting; and they worked together on the *Fistful* soundtrack. This soundtrack turned out to be unlike anything

Morricone (or anyone else, for that matter) had scored before. The tunes were not particularly original (in fact, one can recognize phrases from other Western themes, or from popular tunes of the moment, in Morricone's scores, and he is especially fond of hi-jacking "quotes" from Beethoven and Bach): but the arrangements were extraordinarily appropriate. It was as if Duane Eddy had bumped into Rodrigo, in the middle of a crowded Via Veneto.[10]

Frayling provides a wealth of information about events leading up to the creation of Morricone's score for *A Fistful of Dollars*, but some explanation may be helpful. He is saying that Morricone's earliest scores followed the conventions of film scoring rather closely, but that Leone found Morricone's popular music arrangements much more suit-able for his films. Not only did Leone showcase Morricone's music in his Westerns by giving the music a generous amount of time on the soundtrack, free from excessive dialogue, but he also granted Morri-cone greater creative license, encouraging the composer to break with the film scoring conventions of the time and to incorporate more popu-lar elements.

Without mentioning the instrument by name, Frayling is cleverly referring to Morricone's use of the guitar, both acoustic and electric, in his popular Italian music arrangements. Duane Eddy was an American guitar player who had several hit recordings in the 1950s and 1960s including "Rebel Rouser," "Forty Miles of Bad Road," and "Because They're Young." Joaquín Rodrigo was a Spanish guitarist and com-poser of some of the best-known classical guitar music, including his "Concierto de Aranjuez," which has been heard in American television commercials. Frayling is using this humorous visual image to describe Morricone's synthesis of popular, traditional, and modern elements in his Western scores: an American rock-and-roll guitar player and a Spanish classical guitarist surrounded by the commotion of modern Italian life, as one might find along Via Veneto, a busy street that winds through Rome and is home to some of Rome's most popular hotels, restaurants, and cafés. Frayling's imaginative analogy evokes the cor-rect state of affairs, describing some of the most distinguishing aspects of Morricone's compositional style at the time.

Thus, Morricone found himself in a rare and luxurious position, that of composing music for films in which, because of many scenes with little or no dialogue, his music was able to be heard above all else, and being given the opportunity and encouragement by his director to freely experiment with incorporating popular elements in his scores. This resulted in a very fruitful partnership between Leone and Morricone and the ultimate creation of many of Morricone's most memorable works.

Morricone's Other Early Italian Film Scores

It quickly became apparent just how prolific a film music composer Morricone would be. By the time *The Good, the Bad and the Ugly* was released in Italy in 1966, he had already composed music for over three dozen Italian films, including many Westerns, such as Ricardo Blasco's *Duello nel Texas (Duel in Texas*, a.k.a. *Gunfight at Red Sands)*, Mario Caiano's *Le pistole non discutono (Pistols Don't Argue*, a.k.a. *Bullets Don't Argue)*, Duccio Tessari's *Una pistola per Ringo (A Pistol for Ringo*, a.k.a. *A Gun for Ringo)* and its sequel *Il ritorno di Ringo (The Return of Ringo)*, Franco Giraldi's *Sette pistole per i MacGregor (Seven Pistols for the MacGregors)*, Alberto De Martino's *Centomila dollori per Ringo (One Hundred Thousand Dollars for Ringo)*, and of course the first two Westerns of Sergio Leone, *Per un pugno di dollari (A Fistful of Dollars)* and *Per qualche dollaro in più (For a Few Dollars More)*.

Morricone's scores for Westerns represent the best-known facet of his output. But in addition to his numerous contributions to that genre, his films with Italian directors other than Sergio Leone are also noteworthy. As Royal S. Brown has pointed out:

> Ennio Morricone's collaborations with Sergio Leone represent, of course, only a minuscule portion of his overall career as a film composer. In Italy alone Morricone has also had important collaborations with such directors as Bernardo Bertolucci, Pier Paolo Pasolini, and Marco Bellocchio.[11]

Therefore, by the time Morricone began composing film music in the early 1960s, he not only had a strong classical and modern music education, but also years of experience in the popular music business as an arranger and producer, experience as an orchestral performer, and experience composing music for the stage. He had the means and the opportunity to venture into a realm of film music composition that very few composers have enjoyed, an experimental realm that would eventually become his legacy.

Hollywood

As may be well known, *A Fistful of Dollars* and its two sequels, *For a Few Dollars More* and *The Good, the Bad and the Ugly*, were not released in the United States until 1967 when United Artists, who had already enjoyed great success distributing the British-produced James Bond films in the United States, decided to release Leone's Italian-made Westerns. United Artists eventually released all three Leone Westerns starring Clint Eastwood, making Eastwood an international star almost immediately and giving Morricone's music well-deserved exposure in America. Morricone's film music became quite popular in the United States, and the soundtrack albums for these films, released by United Artists Records, became best-sellers on the American pop album charts.

Hollywood soon recognized the significance of the contributions that Morricone had made to these Westerns. By the beginning of the next decade, Morricone had been recruited to compose scores for Hollywood films as well, beginning with Don Siegel's *Two Mules for Sister Sara* (1970), starring Clint Eastwood. Morricone's first Academy Award nomination was for a Hollywood film, Terrence Malick's *Days of Heaven* (1978). Other Academy Award nominations for Morricone's music for English-language films include director Roland Joffé's *The Mission* (1986), Brian De Palma's *The Untouchables* (1987), and Barry Levinson's *Bugsy* (1991).

Although he has enjoyed success with American films, Morricone has never fully embraced the American film industry, nor has he won an Academy Award. There is little doubt that his decision not to live and work in Hollywood has enabled him to continue composing with a more European perspective, developing a style that is not directly derived from the musical conventions of Hollywood. Living in Rome, he enjoys a level of privacy that a film composer may not be able to find while working in Hollywood. However, Morricone has occasionally spent time in Hollywood when working on American films and, for a short time in the mid-1990s, was a member of the American Federation of Musicians.

His desire to live and work in his beloved Rome is understandable, but this may be more a matter of lifestyle than geography. He has turned down very attractive offers to live and work in Hollywood. The glamorous and fast-paced Hollywood lifestyle seems unsuitable for someone who enjoys having a great deal of time to dedicate to his work and to film music as an art. He obviously enjoys working as much as most Hollywood celebrities enjoy receiving media attention.

Musical Personality

It should not be forgotten that, even though he may be thought of as a composer of film music, the other facets of his sophisticated musical personality are always at hand. As Sweeting observed for *The Guardian*, "Quiz him on his musical roots and he tips his hat to some of the most uncompromising figures of twentieth-century music, including Boulez, Stockhausen, Luciano Berio, and Luigi Nono. Not that he has set out to terrify his listeners with atonal atrocities. It's more a matter of absorption and evolution."[12] Indeed, Morricone's music can be modern and dissonant, but still quite tonal or modal, as well as very melodic at the same time, making it accessible to the average listener as well as the average moviegoer. Yet one need not look far to discover some of these modern elements that he has assimilated, such as the instances of *musique concrète* and suggestions of tonal ambiguity in *The Good, the Bad and the Ugly*.

Even though he continues to experience great success in the music business, Morricone is able to retain the many artistic influences of his classical and modern training. Sergio Miceli, Morricone scholar and colleague, explains this duality:

> He thus developed two distinct sides to his musical personality: one of these led him to embrace serialism (e.g., in *Distanze* and *Musica per 11 violini*, 1958) and the experimental work of the improvisation group Nuova Consonanza (from 1965); the other gained him a leading role, principally as an arranger, in all types of mass-media popular music, including songs for radio, radio and television plays, and the first successful television variety shows. In the early days of the record industry his innovative contribution played a decisive part in the success of the first Italian singer-songwriters ("cantautori"), including Gianni Morandi and Gino Paoli.[13]

These two sides of his personality seem to coexist perfectly, and there is no doubt that one enhances the other. Despite the fact that Morricone has always been best known for the commercially successful side of this personality, and probably always will be, the avant-garde side of this duality, including serialism, minimalism, and other twentieth-century "isms," should not be discounted. These modern elements, which will be discussed in chapter 2, have no doubt contributed to the uniqueness of all of his compositions.

Although his film music career would continue to be the best-known and most recognized facet of his creative output, his nonfilm music should not be overlooked. Miceli emphasizes this fact:

> Morricone's non-film works form a large and increasingly widely performed part of his output. Many of them use his technique of "micro-cells," a pseudo-serial approach often incorporating modal and tonal allusions, which, with its extreme reduction of compositional materials, has much in common with his film-music techniques. His most fruitful season of concert-music composition began with the *Second Concerto* for flute, cello and orchestra (1985, from which the *Cadenza* for flute and tape of 1988 is derived) and continued with *Riflessi* (1989–90), three pieces for cello which represent perhaps the highpoint of his chamber music output, attaining a high degree of lyrical tension.[14]

Morricone's concert music is well-known in Europe and its popularity there appears to be growing. It is indeed unfortunate that his concert music is almost completely unknown in the United States, as it seems to employ many of the same compositional techniques that he uses in his film music. Morricone acknowledges this state of affairs; as he told Joe Gore of *Guitar Player* magazine in 1997, "In my work for the movies, I have never forgotten my classical origins as a composer for concert halls, and I remain a concert composer today. Most of my work is performed here in Europe today, but not, unfortunately, in the States."[15] One can only hope that, in the United States, Morricone's concert music will not continue to be overlooked in favor of his film music, but rather appreciated alongside it.

Morricone's micro-cell technique, which makes the transition from one short musical motive, or "cell," to the next one always logical but perhaps occasionally abrupt, is indeed evident in many of his film scores. Morricone acknowledges that he used this technique in his score for *The Good, the Bad and the Ugly*, but unfortunately, he prefers not to discuss this technique in detail.[16] Although the application of this technique as part of his compositional process will remain somewhat of a mystery, some of the characteristics of the micro-cell technique are evident in his music for *The Good, the Bad and the Ugly*, as will be demonstrated in chapter 5.

The fact that Miceli describes Morricone's micro-cell technique as "pseudo-serial" is significant. In classical serialism, or the so-called twelve-tone method, a composer creates a *tone row* made of the twelve different pitch classes. Composers often divide these twelve pitch classes into groups of three (trichords), four (tetrachords), five (pentachords), or six (hexachords). Part of the compositional process is to arrange these smaller groups in various orders, either consecutively or simultaneously, to achieve different orderings of all twelve pitches (aggregates). By contrast, Morricone's micro-cell technique, which also involves the combination of small groups of pitches, is not restricted in the same ways as classical serialism in that it does not depend on the inclusion of all twelve pitch classes, but can be applied to tonal and modal music as well.

Awards

Throughout his career, Morricone has been nominated for five Academy Awards. His most recent Academy Award nomination was for the Italian-language romance *Malèna* (2000), starring Monica Bellucci, one of several successful collaborations with director Giuseppe Tornatore. Morricone's continued success in these other genres is evidence of his versatility as a film composer. To categorize Morricone only as a composer of music for Westerns is to ignore his innovative contributions to non-Western film genres.

In addition to his Academy Award nominations, he has won Golden Globe Awards for his scores to *The Mission* (1986) and *The Legend of 1900* (1998), as well as a Grammy Award for his score to *The Untouchables* (1987). In Italy, he has won Silver Ribbon Awards for his scores to *A Fistful of Dollars* (1964), *Metti una sera a cena* (1969), *Sacco e Vanzetti* (1971), *Once Upon a Time in America* (1984), *The Untouchables*, *Canone inverso—Making Love* (2000), and *Malèna*. In 1997, at the recommendation of Philip Tagg, an Honorary Doctorate in Music was conferred on Morricone by the Music Department at the University of Liverpool.

Almost all of Morricone's work in recent years has been for Italian films and television. He prefers to live in his hometown of Rome, and he politely insists on speaking and corresponding only in Italian. He and his wife Maria, whom he met in 1950 and married in 1956, have three sons and one daughter: Marco (b. 1957); Alessandra (b. 1961); Andrea (b. 1964), a composer and conductor; and Giovanni (b. 1966), a film director. In recent years, Morricone has collaborated with two of his sons, Andrea and Giovanni, on some film projects.

2

MORRICONE'S TECHNIQUE OF FILM SCORING

If one compares Ennio Morricone's approach to composing film music to that of Hollywood film composers, one might find more differences than similarities. Some of these differences are purely technical while others are much more philosophical. It is the combination of all of these differences that distinguishes Morricone's style from those of his Hollywood contemporaries, such as Elmer Bernstein, Miklós Rózsa, Jerry Goldsmith, and John Williams.

Morricone brings to his film music not only all of the knowledge gained from his classical music education and popular music business experience, but also an admirable work ethic. In Hollywood, the process of composing, arranging, conducting, and producing film music is a complex and well-oiled machine, very much like an assembly line. While a conductor and orchestra are recording the soundtrack to one film, its orchestrator may already be arranging the music for the next film, and its composer is often writing music for the film to be scored after that one. It is more than a craft; it is a fast, efficient, and profitable business. Morricone, however, refuses to work this way. As he told Jon Burlingame and Gary Crowdus of *Cineaste* in 1995:

> Composers in all epochs and all ages, except perhaps this one, for film and other contemporary musical practices, have always written out their own music. I cannot understand why one who calls himself a composer does not finish his own music, and thereby give the final and definitive touch to his composition. This stems from the era of musical theater, where composers hired arrangers to write out the

music because either they did not know how, or were too lazy, or because of the excessive workload. Throughout the history of music, no
composer has had his score written out by someone else. So why
does this occur in film music? I do not understand.[1]

What Morricone is saying, in effect, is that when composing for film,
he employs many of the same traditions and practices that a composer
of concert music would be expected to employ, nurturing each work
from its conception as a musical idea through its maturity as a complete
opus to be performed. This is central to his philosophy of composing,
whether for film or the concert hall. He is the auteur of the music just
as the director is the auteur of the film. Yet, in spite of the fact that
Morricone insists on adding all of the finishing touches himself, he has
been able to produce film scores at an amazing rate, often turning out
over a dozen film scores a year.

Another noticeable difference in Morricone's style is the amount
of music he writes for a film. The first challenge faced by any film
composer is determining which scenes should have music and which
ones should not. This is no small task. Many Hollywood films contain
easily over an hour or two of music, using it as a background to accompany the narrative, almost from beginning to end. Many of the films for
which Morricone has composed, including the Westerns of Sergio
Leone, may have less than an hour of music, leaving most of the film
unaccompanied. The contrast is compounded by the fact that many of
Leone's films are much longer than the average Hollywood films, at
least in their original versions. It is often the absence of music throughout much of a Leone film that makes the entrance of a musical cue
much more noticeable and dramatic. Morricone does not hesitate to use
the silences between musical cues in much the same way that Leone
will use the silences between dialogue and sound effects: to enhance
the impact of the sound when it eventually arrives.

Indeed, it could be said that the absence of music throughout much
of a film, such as *The Good, the Bad and the Ugly*, draws more attention to the music when it is eventually present. According to Morricone, the decision to include or not to include music in a scene is made
through collaboration between the director and the composer. When
asked how he decides what scenes will have music and what scenes
will not, Morricone replied briefly and to the point, "That is the job of
both director and composer, working together. Absolutely! They discuss it."[2] One can only wonder about the content of such discussions

that took place between Leone and Morricone concerning music for *The Good, the Bad and the Ugly*.

"Musical Chameleon"[3]

Morricone is almost always composing. He begins composing early in the morning nearly every day. He often composes more music than is needed for a particular film and then allows the director to choose which cues to include and which ones to leave unused. As Randall Larson observes:

> Morricone went on to score nearly 300 films in just two decades, running the gamut of filmic and musical styles, writing very rapidly and basically following his own inclinations for the sound. Often, instead of synchronizing music directly to the film, Morricone writes a series of themes which he thinks will be fitting, and lets the director choose those he feels will be most appropriate. (Those left over often appear in wholly different films later on.) While many critics object to this approach, it remains apparent that Morricone's music has, nonetheless, contributed remarkably to the films in which it was used.[4]

Actually, Morricone's music has now appeared in nearly 500 films, television programs, and video games, the vast majority of which have been produced in Italy. The fact that some of his film music may have been written years earlier for other projects and not used might offend critics of film music who believe that the film itself should be the composer's sole inspiration. This method of composing is consistent, however, with Morricone's ability to write music in short units that can be connected together to form larger, more complete musical ideas, creating a whole that is greater than the sum of its parts. It is the combination of the most suitable parts that allows him to adapt old or previously unused music to a new film. The fact that his music contributes significantly to the films in which it has appeared, particularly when given a generous amount of time and space as in a Leone Western, is evidence of the effectiveness of this practice. This practice is reminiscent of but much more sophisticated than one used for music to accompany silent films, when short pieces from a library of music would be selected based on the mood desired at that moment. In the case of silent films, unlike sound films, the music selected would often vary from theater to theater and from performance to performance, making a critical analysis impractical.

There are many characteristics of Morricone's music for the Leone Westerns that make his style recognizable, what Morricone calls his own "calligraphy." These various musical elements will be discussed in detail later in this chapter. In addition, there are some obvious similarities in his music for Westerns. As such, it might be expected that Morricone's music would become formulated, predictable, and often self-imitating, but just the opposite is true. Morricone's style may be unmistakable, but, as MacDonald points out:

> As recognizable as many of his film scores are, Morricone's film-music style remains something of a mystery. Like Jerry Goldsmith, Morricone has perfected the art of being a musical chameleon. Although he became internationally renowned for his scores for the Sergio Leone Western trilogy starring Clint Eastwood as the "Man with No Name," Morricone is much more than a Western composer.[5]

Morricone's film scores are undeniably very recognizable to the attentive ear. However, many of his later scores, which lack the foreground presence that is so obvious in the Leone Westerns, may escape the attention of the passive audience member. Indeed, Morricone's chameleon-like ability to write in a number of film genres demonstrates the breadth of his musical vocabulary. MacDonald's comparison of Morricone and Goldsmith with a chameleon no doubt refers to that reptile's ability to change color, and not necessarily to its ability to blend into the background. Morricone can, when called upon, blend seamlessly into the background, but in the Westerns to which MacDonald refers, such was not the case.

Although the film to be discussed here is a Western that is representative of his early work for films, he has achieved critical acclaim for his more recent music for dramas (*The Mission*, 1986; *The Untouchables*, 1987; *Casualties of War*, 1989; and *Bugsy*, 1991), romances (*Malèna*, 2000), and science fiction films (*Mission to Mars*, 2000) as well. Although Goldsmith may share this chameleon-like quality, the similarities between these two composers end there. Like Morricone, Goldsmith has composed successfully in numerous film genres, but he follows the conventions of Hollywood film music practice much more closely than Morricone.

There are many musical elements that make up Morricone's approach to the compositional process. Some of these elements are firmly based in musical tradition, while others are derivative of popular, modern, ethnic, or even ancient musical styles. It is his unique and personal application of those elements that help to define his unmistakable compositional style.

Traditional Elements

Another noteworthy difference between Morricone and his American counterparts is a matter of formal style and musical tradition. Over the years, Hollywood composers have demonstrated a distinct preference for continuing the *leitmotif* tradition that began in German opera of the nineteenth century, and with Richard Wagner in particular. Max Steiner is perhaps most responsible for establishing this tradition in Hollywood, a tradition continued by John Williams, Jerry Goldsmith, and others. Morricone rarely follows such a practice. According to Robert C. Cumbow:

> Morricone doesn't generally write *leitmotif* music in the "So-and-So's Theme" sense, as Rozsa [*sic*], Williams, Bernstein, and other Wagnerians of film music tend to do. His music is more songlike than recitative—tapping, not surprisingly, the Italian operatic tradition (not the German) and running to the repetition of melodic set-pieces (rather than to the commingling of themes or to the purely atmospheric commentary of most film scores).[6]

Often, leitmotifs are intended to enhance the mood already created by the image and the dialogue and are therefore subordinate to them. Such a style of composing is intended to accompany and enhance the action and dialogue on the screen, and not to take the viewer's attention away from the film's narrative. Typically, such underscoring will not be noticeable to the average viewer. Cumbow is correct in pointing out the Italian operatic tradition in Morricone's film scores. Morricone's scores often consist of short musical pieces, very much like a number opera in which choruses, arias, and recitatives are clearly defined, and therefore continue in the tradition of Verdi and Puccini. In the German operatic tradition, by contrast, the music is constantly unfolding and the various sections are not clearly defined, as evident in the music of Wagner.

Morricone's approach gives music the power to do much more than merely accompany a film with leitmotifs. As he told Harlan Kennedy of *American Film* magazine in 1991, "Music in a film must not add emphasis but must give more body and depth to the story, to the characters, to the language that the director has chosen. It must, therefore, say all that the dialogue, image, effects, etc., cannot say."[7] This belief, perhaps more than any other factor, distinguishes Morricone's approach to film music composition from that of nearly every other composer. Indeed, Morricone's music will often create a mood that is in sharp contrast to the visual image, rather than merely creating a mood to complement the image. For a composer to give his music the ability to go so far beyond the image and dialogue already in a film truly breaks with the belief that film music is little more than background music. In fact, Morricone's music can best be described as foreground music. According to Cumbow, "To the often repeated dictum that the best film editing is 'invisible,' there must be a corollary that the best film music is inaudible, or at least unnoticeable, but Leone and Morricone fly in the face of both notions."[8] Morricone's early film music is very noticeable, and many of the best examples of this foreground quality, with its brilliant timbres and dynamic intensity, can be found in his music for *The Good, the Bad and the Ugly*, as will be seen in chapter 5.

As bold and descriptive as his film music may be, Morricone also brings a certain modesty to the compositional process. He acknowledges that film music is not often held in very high regard and he is quick to express his opinion as to how and why this has taken place. As he told Burlingame and Crowdus:

Film music is not at the same level as classical or chamber music because those compositions are born naturally from the composer himself. The composition expresses itself without any conditions or limitations. In the cinema, the music is conditioned by the images and by the direction of the director, and therefore is complementary to the film. This does not mean that film music is not worthwhile. It always depends on who's writing it. It's not seriously considered because there is a grave infiltration, throughout the entire world, including America, of amateurs and dilettantes, people who do not know music. Therefore, this lowers the level of the profession, and film music is not considered a serious art form.[9]

Morricone's respect for composers of classical and chamber music is admirable, but not surprising considering his classical training and his accomplishments as a composer of concert music. His sharp criticism of those who lower the level of film music by writing what he clearly considers inferior music demonstrates his belief that film music, which should be held in the same high regard as the classical masterpieces, has been diluted by the uneducated and the unprofessional. It is his methodology as a composer of concert music, nurturing his work from its conception through its performance, that has helped to define his contribution to the art of film music. If this "grave infiltration" of amateurs has lowered the artistic level of film music, then undoubtedly the contributions of Morricone, and a small number of other concert music composers (including Sergei Prokofiev, Aaron Copland, and Miklós Rózsa), have helped to elevate the art of film music to a level approaching that of concert music.

In addition to the concert music composers already mentioned, film music composers come from a wide variety of other musical backgrounds. These include, but are not limited to, musical theater (Max Steiner), television (Jerry Goldsmith and John Williams), jazz (John Barry and Quincy Jones), and popular music (Elton John and Randy Newman). Not only has this synthesis of various musical styles into film music helped to redefine the term "film music composer," but it has also had an effect on the film music audience, cultivating a more educated listener than, for example, popular music alone. As will be seen, Morricone's successful incorporation of popular elements into his film music has contributed to its appeal and commercial success, while maintaining its admiration among musicians and scholars.

Popular Elements

Part of Morricone's philosophy that makes it possible for his music to give more body and depth to a story is his desire to present his music in a form that is easily accessible to the average audience member. Jeff Smith explains, "He believed that for film music to communicate with its audience, it was necessary to work in styles, forms, and genres that were already familiar."[10] To put it briefly, many of the same qualities that made the rock-and-roll of the 1960s commercially successful did the same for Morricone's film music: it was concise, easily remembered, easily recognized, harmonically and formally uncomplicated, yet melodically very original.

The Electric Guitar

Morricone's scores, particularly the Westerns of the 1960s including *The Good, the Bad and the Ugly*, demonstrate a fusion of many of the popular music elements of the time. The immense popularity of the electric guitar is the best example of this fusion. Often ignored by Hollywood composers of music for Westerns before the 1960s, the electric guitar may have seemed like an obvious choice for any composer seeking a popular music audience at that time. Although it would be illogical to think of the electric guitar as an instrument that would exist in the world of the old American West, its association with popular music of the modern American cowboy was well established by the time moviegoers first heard Morricone's music in the Leone Westerns of the 1960s.

Musicologist Philip Tagg describes how the English band The Shadows successfully incorporated the sound of a Fender electric guitar into their hits in the early 1960s, many of which had programmatic titles depicting the old American West.

> The Shadows had already attempted to reconcile their clean Fender sound to images of the Wild West with *Apache* in 1960 and seem to have been successful in the process. . . . The Shadows were followed by the The Ramrods, whose successful 1961 cover of the 1949 hit *Ghost Riders in the Sky* demonstrated that even U.S. listeners were becoming receptive to the notion of electric guitar cowboys.[11]

Therefore, the electric guitar sound, which had already been assimilated into the popular country and western music of the mid-twentieth century in the form of the so-called electric guitar cowboys, found a new and larger audience in the popular rock-and-roll of the 1960s. Cumbow explains how this phenomenon took place in the United States, almost simultaneously, also using the hit tune "Apache," covered by Jorgen Ingmann, as an example:

> Another influence on Morricone was the popular guitar instrumentals of the early '60s. When Danny Peary mentioned to me, once, the similarity between Morricone's lilting/galloping Western themes and

an old tune by the Tornadoes (c. 1962), the comparison set in motion a train of thought. The twangy "California Sound" was popular in Europe at the time of Morricone's apprenticeship, and widely imitated by European pop groups. A few guitar instrumentals from the period offer particularly striking examples of the kind of sound Morricone adapted for his Western scores: "Walk, Don't Run" (The Ventures, August, 1960), "Apache" (Jorgen Ingman [sic], March, 1961), "Ridin' the Wind" and several others from the Tornadoes album *Telstar* (December, 1962), "Pipeline" (The Chantays, April, 1963), and "Moon Child" and other cuts on the Ventures' *Out of Limits* album (1964). All predate or are contemporary with Morricone's first Western scores, and the similarity is readily apparent.[12]

Undeniably, there is some similarity between these rock-and-roll instrumental hits of the 1960s and Morricone's use of the solo electric guitar in his Western scores of the same period. Also significant is the fact that Morricone's use of that instrument in his Western scores closely coincides with its use in the "James Bond Theme" heard in *Dr. No*, which was released in the United States on 8 May 1963. The "James Bond Theme" is credited to Monty Norman, but British jazz musician and composer John Barry, who was hired by United Artists late in the production of *Dr. No*, was also involved in the final version of that familiar theme.[13] By the end of the 1960s, therefore, the electric guitar had established itself as an indispensable part of the modern film soundtrack. That Morricone contributed to that process, by his use of that instrument in his Western scores, is indisputable.

Morricone explained his approach to composing for the guitar, both acoustic and electric, to Joe Gore of *Guitar Player* magazine:

When somebody writes music, they are not looking for reasons. One writes a score to attain a certain result. In the search for these results, I have used the electric guitar and its vast range of interesting tones. The guitar is unique among instruments because there is the option to use the traditional acoustic guitar or the electric guitar and the many tones it can offer today.[14]

This statement provides valuable insight into Morricone's basic philosophy on the compositional process. He clearly sees the guitar, or any instrument, as a means to an end, the end being the musical result that he, or any other composer, seeks to achieve. In the case of *The Good, the Bad and the Ugly*, he uses the acoustic guitar as a signifier of things derivative of the southwestern American culture, as he also uses the mariachi trumpet. His use of the electric guitar in that film adds an unexpected vibrancy and energy to the cues in which it appears. He obviously enjoys writing for guitar because of its inherent versatility. His fondness for that instrument, and its subsequent use in his film scores, is an integral part of his overall contribution to the art of film music.

There is little doubt that Morricone initially became familiar with the electric guitar's musical and commercial potential through his years of experience in the Italian music business, arranging many pop tunes for RCA. The fact that Morricone was able to assimilate the electric guitar into his film scores demonstrates his remarkable ability to seamlessly join dissimilar musical elements, the combination of which may seem unconventional at first, particularly to those accustomed to the more homogenous sound of the large studio orchestras of Hollywood.

The Human Voice

Another sound that Morricone was able to successfully integrate into his film music was that of the human voice. Unlike the classical Hollywood film scores that used voices, Morricone would use the voice as an instrument, without words, to add a desired tone color to a melody or to emphasize a particular rhythmic idea. Morricone is surprised that more composers do not do the same. As he told Burlingame and Crowdus:

> The human voice is at the disposal of all composers. Why don't others use it? I love the human voice, because it is an extraordinary instrument. It doesn't go through a piece of wood or metal, it comes directly out of the body and can be the most expressive and malleable instrument. It can react in many strange ways. First, I used the human voice because I love it; and second, I used it because I had an exceptional voice [Edda Dell'Orso] at my disposal. . . . So I became known as someone who uses the human voice all the time. Perhaps it's true, but everyone can use the voice. It's at every composer's disposal.[15]

Morricone's use of the human voice as an instrument is evident in the Leone Westerns and in his score for *The Good, the Bad and the Ugly* in particular, as shall be discussed in chapter 5. He uses the solo female voice melodically as he would a flute, trumpet, or English horn. He also uses a male chorus without words to accentuate more rhythmic ideas, almost as a percussion instrument. Although he may not have originated the practice of writing for the human voice without words in film music (Miklós Rózsa used it in *The Thief of Bagdad* in 1939), the fact that Morricone effectively incorporated this device into his film music is yet another aspect of his contribution to the art. As will be seen, the only time he uses voices with lyrics in *The Good, the Bad and the Ugly* is when the music is *diegetic*, coming from a source known to exist in the world created by the film's narrative, as in the case of the Confederate soldiers who sing while being held prisoner by the Union army.

The Soundtrack Album's Commercial Appeal

Morricone was one of several film music composers of the 1960s to incorporate elements of popular music into their film scores. Not only did this make film music more accessible to the moviegoing public, but it gave the soundtrack album the potential for greater commercial success. According to Jeff Smith:

> *Breakfast at Tiffany's, Goldfinger, The Good, the Bad and the Ugly*, and other films revealed that pop music might be used in ways that satisfied a film's dramatic requirements. Working with different compositional strategies and untraditional musical forms, composers Mancini, Barry, Morricone, Francis Lai, Lalo Schifrin, and Quincy Jones were able to do what had appeared to be impossible only ten or twenty years earlier: they created music in popular idioms that enhanced emotions and moods, cued characters and settings, and signified psychological states and points of view.[16]

To say that Morricone created film music in a "popular idiom" may be an oversimplification. He did not write pop songs per se, rather, he successfully incorporated into his film music many of the elements of the popular styles of the time. Like pop songs, his film music has enjoyed some exposure through radio airplay of cover versions by well-known recording artists, Hugo Montenegro in particular. Morricone's film scores, including those for his early work in Westerns, continue to experience success as commercially available soundtrack albums. There is little doubt that these popular music elements have contributed to that success.

All of these popular music influences—the electric guitar and the human voice as well as the acoustic guitar, harmonica, and exotic percussion instruments—placed Morricone's music in a new category that was both film music and popular music, enabling it to be more easily assimilated into the public's collective consciousness. That his music can exist as both is no doubt what has helped to make many of his movie themes so easily recognizable.

Typically, the soundtrack recordings of many Hollywood Westerns of the 1940s, 1950s, and 1960s were not intended to be popular music. With the Westerns of Leone, and Morricone's music, this changed rapidly. As Russell Lack explains:

> The most radical paradigm change in the musical treatment of the Western genre stemmed from the fertile creative partnership between Italian director Sergio Leone and Ennio Morricone. . . . It was with his first score for Sergio Leone, *A Fistful of Dollars* (1964), that Morricone announced himself as a formidable presence. . . . Certainly Leone's reputation as a musical director, carefully planning the function of music within each scene, and his generosity with space on the soundtrack set Morricone's music in an ideal frame, foregrounding the music's sonic impact as opposed to the emotional.[17]

One important aspect of the relationship between Leone and Morricone was the generous amount of time and space that Morricone's music was given in the Westerns. There are many scenes with little or no dialogue, giving the music the opportunity to be heard above other sounds. When other sounds do occur, such as animal sounds, gunshots, cannon fire, and bugle calls, they are often incorporated into the music and not situated against it. To describe his music as having "sonic impact" is not surprising, considering the foreground presence it achieves through its brilliant and varied tone colors and unprecedented dynamics. His music for these Westerns would almost immediately influence composers of music for American films of that genre. As Gary Marmorstein points out:

> What made Morricone's score distinctive for *A Fistful of Dollars*—and the scores for its descendants, *[For] A Few Dollars More* (1965), *The Good, the Bad and the Ugly* (1967), and *Once Upon a Time in the West* (1969)—was its variety of crisscrossing themes, which owed more to the hi-fi exotica recorded by the likes of Martin Denny

and Les Baxter than to anyone's idea of Americana. Morricone liked to isolate a character with a single instrument—the trumpet, of course, was the one he used most, though he famously used the harmonica in *Once Upon a Time in the West* for Charles Bronson's character—obscuring the fact that his ensembles were usually as large as American studio orchestras. The Morricone sound became so influential that audiences mistakenly assumed he'd scored *Hang 'Em High* (1968), Clint Eastwood's and director Ted Post's Hollywood version of the spaghetti Western. The twangy score was by Dominic Frontiere.[18]

The fact that Morricone's style became imitated by Hollywood composers demonstrates how seriously the Hollywood film industry took the commercial success of these Italian films and their European-influenced music. His style, which was distinctive for its time in its use of various popular elements, profoundly influenced other composers. Morricone's innovations, many of which are evident in *The Good, the Bad and the Ugly*, would eventually become part of many composers' musical vocabulary. As MacDonald observes:

> With its vocal yells and grunts, *The Good, the Bad and the Ugly* theme seemed to redefine the sound of film music. Its raucous, brash, and rhythmically driven sound departed drastically from the folksy style of Dimitri Tiomkin's Western ballads and the exuberant full-orchestra sonorities of Elmer Bernstein. Morricone suddenly became the established master of Western film music and, although he would later branch out into other genres, his Western themes would remain his chief claim to fame.[19]

That Morricone's music is easily distinguished from that of Tiomkin, Bernstein, and others is further indication of his contribution to film music. MacDonald is correct is describing Morricone's Western scores as his "chief claim to fame," but it is perhaps unfortunate that his Western themes have become so much better known than his work in other film genres. Their success has no doubt taken some attention away from his many other significant cinematic accomplishments.

Furthermore, it should be mentioned that in spite of all the innovations in Morricone's film scores that distinguished them from other Western scores—the vibrant electric guitar, the wordless soprano melodies, and the exotic and unexpected percussion—in many ways he would often follow some of the well-established conventions of the genre. As Jeff Smith has argued, Morricone's approach embraces traditional nonfilmic compositional strategies, such as key organization and motivic unity. However, Smith's description of the "parameters of tempo, dynamics, texture, and tone color"[20] as "secondary"[21] is to underestimate their position in the hierarchy of a Morricone film score. Morricone's demonstrated preference for sonic presence places significant importance on just these parameters.

For example, key relationships and the harmonic and rhythmic techniques used in *The Good, the Bad and the Ugly*, which will be discussed in chapter 5, are actually quite conservative. His use of texture and tone color create as much variety in a score as harmonic progressions and changes of key would create in the hands of a Hollywood composer.

Morricone's use of the string orchestra, for example, can be considered very traditional, as he employs few special effects for strings. Also, the formal unity of his music is an essential element, as it helps to keep all of the other, less traditional elements in perspective and in a context that the audience can easily understand. In other words, by using simple key relationships and primarily diatonic harmony, the audience is not overwhelmed by his unusual choices of instruments and vocal effects.

Modern Elements

The duality that exists between the commercial and modern sides of Morricone's musical personality was discussed in chapter 1. Many of the modern compositional practices that make up Morricone's modern side are evident in his music for *The Good, the Bad and the Ugly*. For example, the cue "The Desert" is noticeably the most tonally ambiguous cue in the score. Its use of eleven different pitch classes in the English horn solo (figure 5.5) suggests the inclusion of serialism, a method that, in its purest form, systematically gives equal emphasis to all twelve pitch classes as a means of avoiding the establishment of a tonal center. Although Morricone seems to suggest the key of A minor by the use of the A minor piano ostinato, the effect on the listener is one of uncertainty where the cue's true tonality is concerned.

The repeated ostinatos in "The Desert" (figures 5.6 and 5.7), as well as in "The Rope Bridge" (figure 5.4), "The Ecstasy of Gold" (figure 5.17), and "The Trio" (figure 5.20), reflect a strong influence of minimalism, the practice of basing a composition almost entirely on the extensive repetition of a short musical idea, the slightest alteration of which becomes very noticeable and dramatic. Although minimalism was used in later film scores, particularly those of Philip Glass (*Koyaanisqatsi*, 1983), such a device was still quite rare in the 1960s and is evidence of Morricone's inclusion of modern elements in his film music.

Another modern technique that Morricone employs is that of musique concrète, a twentieth-century compositional technique in which composers add nonmusical sounds—including natural sounds, such as animal noises or the sound of a waterfall, as well as mechanical or man-made sounds—to more conventional musical sounds. One example of musique concrète is the mechanical pocket-watch motif heard in *For a Few Dollars More* (figure 2.9), which Morricone seamlessly blends into his orchestration. Another example is the sounds of crows heard in *The Good, the Bad and the Ugly*, immediately following the first trumpet solo in "The Trio" (figure 5.21). An even more striking use of musique concrète occurs in the opening sequence of *Once Upon a Time in the West*, where mechanical and natural sounds (a waterwheel, a telegraph, and dripping water), with no other musical accompaniment, become musical through the emphasis that is given to their own inherent rhythmic motifs.

Ethnic and Ancient Elements

Morricone has gone far beyond merely assimilating many of the sounds of popular and modern music. For example, he acknowledges that his use of minor keys, displaying a distinct preference for the natural form of the minor scale or the Aeolian mode, is similar to that of traditional Celtic music.[22] He frequently will use a minor scale and raise the sixth scale degree a semitone, not the seventh scale degree as is common in harmonic minor. This results in a scale that is called the Dorian mode, a scale which can be traced back to Gregorian chant (figure 2.1).

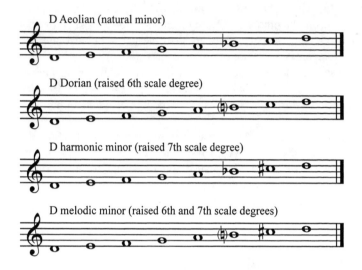

Figure 2.1: Minor and Dorian Scales

Many of Morricone's melodies for Western films omit the sixth scale degree altogether, giving those melodies a certain ambiguity concerning their true mode. The result is a minor hexatonic scale that may be perceived as being either Aeolian or Dorian in origin (figure 2.2).

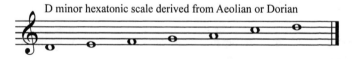

Figure 2.2: Minor Hexatonic Scale

One example of this minor hexatonic scale can be found in the melody of the "Main Title" from *A Fistful of Dollars* (figure 2.3),[23] which is in D minor or D Dorian, the sixth scale degree (B or B-flat) being noticeably absent. This familiar melody features the human whistle (performed by virtuoso whistler and guitarist Alessandro Alessandroni), a timbre that Morricone used in many of his themes for Westerns, including the two subsequent Sergio Leone Westerns that starred Clint Eastwood. This theme is accompanied by a soprano recorder playing a five-note ostinato (a descending D minor scale from A to D) that Miceli describes as "quasi l'evocazione di un glissando sulle cinque canne di un flauto di Pan . . . affidato a un flauto diritto soprano soffiato più che suonato . . ."[24] (similar to a glissando on a five-piped Pan flute . . . entrusted to a soprano recorder, blown rather than played . . .). This five-note ostinato is likewise derived from the D minor hexatonic scale on which the theme is based.

Figure 2.3: "Main Title"
from *A Fistful of Dollars* by Ennio Morricone

The melody of the A section of the "Main Title" from *The Good, the Bad and the Ugly* (figure 5.1) is based on the same D minor hexatonic scale. Similarly, the melody of the cue "The Ecstasy of Gold" (figure 5.18) is based on a minor hexatonic scale on A, as will be seen in chapter 5.

The "Main Title" from *For a Few Dollars More* (figure 2.4),[25] however, is clearly in D minor as it includes both C-sharps and C-naturals, as well as an occasional B-natural. As in the melodic minor scale, where the sixth and seventh degrees are raised in the ascending form but not in the descending form, C-sharp ascends to D, but C-natural descends.

Moderato

Figure 2.4: "Main Title"
from *For A Few Dollars More* by Ennio Morricone
© 1967 (Renewed) Edizioni Eureka (Italy)
Rights for the world outside Italy controlled by U.S. Music International, Inc.
Rights in the U.S.A. and Canada administered by EMI Unart Catalog Inc. (Publishing)
and Warner Bros. Publications Inc. (Print)
All Rights Reserved. Used by Permission.
WARNER BROS. PUBLICATIONS U.S. INC., Miami, FL 33014

Tagg has made a similar observation about Morricone's fluency with the minor modes of Aeolian and Dorian and their roles in creating a sound that is distinct from the classical western European sound found in many Hollywood film scores. Morricone explains Tagg's theory in his own words:

Tagg, a musicologist who teaches at the University of Liverpool [now at the University of Montréal], has a theory with which I fully concur. He states that some of my musical compositions written for cinema, and also for Westerns, have what is called a Celtic "modality." I would further add that the same can be said for Gregorian chants, which have also influenced my cinematographic soundtracks.[26]

It is truly remarkable that Morricone, who can be extremely elusive when asked to acknowledge any influences whatsoever on his compositional style, would confirm the influence of Celtic music and Gregorian chants in his cinematic music for Westerns. This demonstrates the extent of his musical vocabulary while demystifying much of his enigmatic compositional process. As innovative as he is at times, he acknowledges that some innovations are rooted in influences from the distant past. Morricone has made use of the Dorian mode in many of his themes for Westerns, including, as will be seen in chapter 5, the "Main Title" from *The Good, the Bad and the Ugly*.[27] His skill at seamlessly adapting some of the characteristics of medieval music into his Western film scores demonstrates the versatility of his technique.

Another ethnic element that Morricone has effectively incorporated into his compositional style, for Westerns in particular, is the mariachi-style solo trumpet. Traditionally Mexican in nature, this style of trumpet playing remains popular in Mexico and the southwestern United States today. Cumbow describes Morricone's use of this particular trumpet style: "The mariachi trumpet air is another convention to which Morricone gave new life. In fact, through a series of Italian Western scores, he made this convention virtually his own."[28] These solos, always reserved for the film's final confrontation between good and evil, add a masculine and, at the same time, southwestern American characteristic to the film's climax. It could be argued that Morricone's fondness for this instrument originates in the fact that both he and his father were trumpeters. This may in fact be the case, but the trumpet is also a logical choice for these confrontational scenes by virtue of its energetic and dominating presence.

Morricone's choice of tonality for these solos is also noteworthy. The mariachi trumpet solo from *A Fistful of Dollars* (figure 2.5)[29] is clearly in D minor as it includes all seven notes of that diatonic scale.[30] The F-sharp in the sixth measure is a chromatic note. Although Morricone's themes for the main titles of Leone's Westerns are diatonic, each of Morricone's mariachi-style trumpet solos includes one chromatic note: the F-sharp in the solo heard in *A Fistful of Dollars*, the G-sharp in the solo heard in *For a Few Dollars More* (figure 2.6), and the F-sharp heard in the solo from *The Good, the Bad and the Ugly* (figure 5.21). The introduction of the F-sharp embellishes G, while the G-sharp in *For a Few Dollars More* has the same ornamental effect on A.

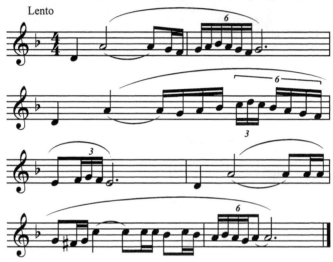

Figure 2.5: "Trumpet Solo"
from *A Fistful of Dollars* by Ennio Morricone
© 1964 (Renewed) Edizioni Eureka (Italy)
Rights for the world outside Italy controlled by U.S. Music International, Inc.
Rights in the U.S.A. and Canada administered by EMI Unart Catalog Inc. (Publishing)
and Warner Bros. Publications Inc. (Print)
All Rights Reserved. Used by Permission.
WARNER BROS. PUBLICATIONS U.S. INC., Miami, FL 33014

The mariachi trumpet solo that is heard at the climax of *For a Few Dollars More* (figure 2.6)[31] is also clearly in D minor, but uses the natural form of the scale, as it includes B-flats and one C-natural. The G-sharp in the fifth measure is a chromatic note, similar to the chromatic note in figure 2.5.

Figure 2.6: "Trumpet Solo"
from *For A Few Dollars More* by Ennio Morricone
© 1967 (Renewed) Edizioni Eureka (Italy)
Rights for the world outside Italy controlled by U.S. Music International, Inc.
Rights in the U.S.A. and Canada administered by EMI Unart Catalog Inc. (Publishing)
and Warner Bros. Publications Inc. (Print)
All Rights Reserved. Used by Permission.
WARNER BROS. PUBLICATIONS U.S. INC., Miami, FL 33014

These mariachi-style trumpet solos are distinguished from Morricone's other uses of the solo trumpet by their noticeably wide and fast vibrato, their brilliant and piercing tone, and by a style of articulation that makes the beginning and ending of each note more intense and abrupt than in other styles of trumpet playing. By contrast, Morricone also uses the solo trumpet, played with a much more orchestral style, for many of his most majestic themes, such as "The Strong" and "The Carriage of the Spirits" in *The Good, the Bad and the Ugly*. He has continued to feature the solo trumpet, without its distinctive mariachi character, in many of his later film scores as well, including *The Untouchables* and *Malèna*.

The trumpet solo from *A Fistful of Dollars* is noteworthy for another reason. It begins with the interval of an ascending fifth from tonic to dominant. Morricone will often begin his minor-mode themes with this interval. In addition to this trumpet melody from *A Fistful of Dollars*, he does so in the cues "The Vice of Killing" from *For a Few Dollars More* (figure 2.7), "The Ecstasy of Gold" from *The Good, the Bad and the Ugly* (figure 5.18), and "Man with a Harmonica" from *Once Upon a Time in the West*.

Figure 2.7: "The Vice of Killing"
from *For A Few Dollars More* by Ennio Morricone
© 1967 (Renewed) Edizioni Eureka (Italy)
Rights for the world outside Italy controlled by U.S. Music International, Inc.
Rights in the U.S.A. and Canada administered by EMI Unart Catalog Inc. (Publishing)
and Warner Bros. Publications Inc. (Print)
All Rights Reserved. Used by Permission.
WARNER BROS. PUBLICATIONS U.S. INC., Miami, FL 33014

"The Vice of Killing" in *For a Few Dollars More*, like "The Carriage of the Spirits" in *The Good, the Bad and the Ugly* (figure 5.8), demonstrates Morricone's ability to create a moving theme with a limited number of pitches. Not only can these melodies be derived from the minor hexatonic scale, but they are in fact pentatonic, omitting both the second and sixth notes of the minor scale.

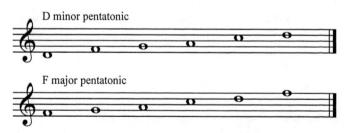

Figure 2.8: Pentatonic Scales

The resulting minor-mode pentatonic scale actually consists of the same five pitches that constitute the traditional major pentatonic scale in F, the relative major of D minor.

Transcending the Diegesis

For the most part, the music that Morricone composes for films is non-diegetic, coming from a source that the audience understands is not part of the world created by the film's story. In *The Good, the Bad and the Ugly*, there are a few instances of diegetic music. Morricone will, however, occasionally cross that fine line that exists between a film's diegesis and the nondiegetic world, disrupting the audience's perception concerning the source of the music. In *For a Few Dollars More*, for example, there is a recurring musical motif, also in D minor, that is heard originating from the identical pocket-watches that El Indio and Colonel Mortimer carry with them (figure 2.9). The sound of these musical chimes, when first heard, is diegetic. The audience sees and hears a pocket-watch. Morricone enhances this motif with nondiegetic instruments until the sound of the chimes is almost inaudible.

Figure 2.9: "Pocket-Watch Chimes"
from *For A Few Dollars More* by Ennio Morricone
© 1967 (Renewed) Edizioni Eureka (Italy)
Rights for the world outside Italy controlled by U.S. Music International, Inc.
Rights in the U.S.A. and Canada administered by EMI Unart Catalog Inc. (Publishing)
and Warner Bros. Publications Inc. (Print)
All Rights Reserved. Used by Permission.
WARNER BROS. PUBLICATIONS U.S. INC., Miami, FL 33014

The audience understands the source of the chimes exists in the world created by the film, but the accompanying instruments obviously do not. The effect on the viewer is somewhat unsettling, which is no doubt what Morricone had in mind.

Similar chimes are heard in *The Good, the Bad and the Ugly* during the interlude of the cue "The Trio" (figure 5.22), which occurs at that film's climactic confrontation. In that cue, the chime motif is clearly nondiegetic, yet it is unmistakably reminiscent of the diegetic chimes that are heard in the climax of *For a Few Dollars More*.

The line separating the diegetic and nondiegetic world is blurred once again in the cue "Short March" (figure 5.11). Prisoners of war are seen marching as the theme is heard being played on the harmonica, and later whistling is heard as well. It is reasonable to assume that a harmonica player could be present, but none is seen. Likewise it is possible that the prisoners are whistling, but when the audience briefly sees the prisoner's faces, none are whistling, yet they are obviously marching in perfect time with the music. Is the source of the music coming from within the world created by Leone's film? The synchronized marching of the prisoners leads the audience to believe so, but no source of this music is visible in the film, it is only assumed.

Shortly after the "Short March," military bugle calls are heard from within the prison camp (figures 5.12 and 5.13). Since it is logical to assume that a bugler would be present at the camp and would be playing these calls, one must conclude that these calls are diegetic. However, no bugler is visible to the audience. Once again the audience must place these sounds with the film's diegesis even though their source remains unseen.

Morricone also crosses the line separating the diegetic and nondiegetic worlds with the cue "The Story of a Soldier" (figure 5.14) in *The Good, the Bad and the Ugly*. That song is originally sung by characters known to exist in the world created by the film, but is heard later in the film, in its vocal form, with voices that can only be nondiegetic. Tuco (Eli Wallach) has jumped off a train in the middle of the desert with Corporal Wallace (Mario Brega) and has just killed him. The voices singing cannot possibly exist diegetically.

In Morricone's score for *Once Upon a Time in the West*, the sound of the harmonica is often nondiegetic. When it is diegetic, being played by Charles Bronson's character, the harmonica is often heard before it is seen, making its source, at least temporarily, ambiguous.

Later Works

Since the Westerns of Sergio Leone, Morricone's compositional style for his film music has continued to evolve, as he is always seeking new and innovative ways to synthesize elements from different musical genres into a sound that is uniquely his own. His recent work includes artistically and commercially successful collaborations with Italian director Giuseppe Tornatore (*Cinema Paradiso*, 1989; and *Malèna*, 2000) and American director Brian De Palma (*The Untouchables*, 1987; *Casualties of War*, 1989; and *Mission to Mars*, 2000). If one compares

Morricone's style and technique that is evident in the Sergio Leone films of the 1960s and 1970s to his more recent work, it could be said that his later scores depend less on thematic material and more on the creation of a desired mood or effect through the sophisticated manipulation of timbre and dynamics. His unusual orchestration may not be as obvious to the casual listener, but it is always present. His recent scores, as complex and well-thought-out as they are, lack the foreground presence that is so obvious in his earlier music for Westerns. Also, the later films are usually much shorter in length than the Leone films, leaving less time for Morricone's music to be heard over dialogue and sound effects.

It could further be acknowledged that his earlier works are more thematic, employing themes as signifiers of people or things in a way similar to, but easily distinguished from, the leitmotif technique employed by Max Steiner. Morricone's later works, therefore, could be compared more closely to the style of Bernard Herrmann, which depends on the creation of the desired mood by the use of pitch, tone color, and repetition much more so than on recognizable themes. Morricone has recently commented on his use of themes, as opposed to the creation of a desired mood without an easily identifiable melody:

> Personally, I can do without a melodic theme. In fact, in many cases I have tried to disguise the melodic theme within rests, pauses, and silence, and to encourage the public to identify those sentimental sensations with musical colors instead of a theme. Unfortunately, even though I've conducted many experiments along these lines, the public still wants to hear a melody.[32]

This serves as a reminder that Morricone, who could easily continue composing with methods that have proven successful in the past, instead chooses to experiment continuously with the public's perception of his music. In effect, he is saying that he composes melodies because that is what the public wants, or more specifically, that is what the public believes it needs in order to understand the sensations already experienced in a film.

One of Morricone's nonfilm experiments in disguising a theme using these methods is his *Esercizi per dieci archi* (*Exercises for Ten String Soloists*), composed in 1992 and 1993. The melody is from the aria "Amami, Alfredo" from Giuseppe Verdi's *La Traviata*. The piece, which bears little resemblance to Morricone's film music, renders the

melody almost unrecognizable through its rhythmic variation and inclusion of numerous rests.

To summarize, Morricone's compositional style is an eclectic
blend of musical traditions synthesized with many of the elements of
the popular and modern music of his time. He acknowledges a debt to
the great classical composers, while at the same time he continues some
of the conventions of the classic Hollywood film scores, and yet he
does not hesitate to incorporate into his scores elements from all other
musical styles—medieval, popular, ethnic, or avant-garde—to achieve
the desired musical and cinematic goal.

3

HISTORICAL AND CRITICAL CONTEXT OF
THE GOOD, THE BAD AND THE UGLY

The previous chapters discussed Morricone's diverse musical experiences and many of his compositional techniques that helped to make
his score for *The Good, the Bad and the Ugly* distinctive for its time.
This chapter is intended to place that film in a historical context so that
the reader will gain an understanding of the film and its music from the
perspective of the American moviegoing public of the 1960s. There
were many cultural, social, and political issues that affected the collective consciousness of the American public at the time. Not only did this
collective consciousness affect the viewing experience of this film, but
this film in turn marked the collective consciousness of Americans who
have seen it, not only through its graphic depiction of war and violence,
but through Morricone's memorable music as well.

Cultural Context

Il buono, il brutto, il cattivo (The Good, the Bad and the Ugly) was
released in Italy on 23 December 1966 but was not released in the
United States until 29 December 1967, slightly more than a year later.
The two previous "Dollar" films, *Per un pugno di dollari (A Fistful of
Dollars)*[1] and *Per qualche dollaro in più (For a Few Dollars More)*,
were also released in the United States in 1967.

    Nineteen sixty-seven was a turbulent year in the United States, as
well as in the rest of the world. Lyndon B. Johnson was president, and
the U.S. military and its allies were deeply involved in the Vietnam
War. The space race between the United States and the Soviet Union,

which would land a man on the moon two years later, was increasingly tense; and the so-called British Invasion continued to sweep America, exemplified by the Beatles' release of *Sgt. Pepper's Lonely Hearts Club Band* in the summer of 1967, the "Summer of Love."

Earlier that year, Americans tuned in to watch the first Super Bowl, in which the National Football League champions, the Green Bay Packers, beat the American Football League champions, the Kansas City Chiefs. In baseball, the Saint Louis Cardinals beat the Boston Red Sox to win the 1967 World Series.

In Hollywood that year, the Academy Award for best picture went to *In the Heat of the Night*, with the other nominees being *Bonnie and Clyde*, *Doctor Dolittle*, *The Graduate*, and *Guess Who's Coming to Dinner*. A Western had not been nominated as best picture since 1962's *How the West Was Won*. In spite of the apparently waning popularity of the Western in America, United Artists believed that these Westerns had marketability. According to Jeff Smith, "UA hoped to market the *Dollar* films along the lines of its James Bond series and created a timetable calculated to build interest for its Christmas release of the third film, now titled *The Good, the Bad and the Ugly*."[2] United Artists followed through with their plans and released *The Good, the Bad and the Ugly* late in 1967.

Synopsis

Set against the beautiful, colorful, and breathtaking landscapes of the old American West, which were actually filmed in Spain, *The Good, the Bad and the Ugly*, with its gritty, violent, and amoral protagonists, had a strange and perhaps unexpected popularity with American audiences. Edward Gallafent explains how this film compares to the previous two Leone Westerns:

> A number of other characteristics distinguish *The Good, the Bad and the Ugly* from the earlier Dollars films. In part, it is an exercise in the representation of the specific historical period of the American Civil War rather than a more general evocation of the western landscape— again the increased budget was no doubt instrumental in making this a possibility. It is hardly interested at all in the histories of its characters, or actions that spring from or depend on pieties seen to be learned from another time. Rather, it is an account of behaviour based

on a calculation of immediate gain—a caper movie. And where other comedy Westerns refer back to the history of Western production through the use of major stars, Leone plays with a smaller but related canvas, exploiting the audience's assumed knowledge of the earlier Dollars movies.[3]

It is the audience's knowledge of those earlier films, and hence its familiarity with Clint Eastwood's on-screen persona, along with a higher advertising and production budget, that propelled *The Good, the Bad and the Ugly* to greater box office success in the United States than its two predecessors. The audience's prior knowledge of the "man with no name" character and his amoral set of values almost certainly influenced their expectations of Eastwood's character in this film.

Briefly, *The Good, the Bad and the Ugly* tells the story of three gunslingers, Blondie (Clint Eastwood), Tuco (Eli Wallach), and Angel Eyes (Lee Van Cleef), who earn their living as hired killers or who use their skills to collect reward money fraudulently. The central plot of the film reveals itself when the protagonists each discover the secret of a buried cashbox containing two hundred thousand dollars in gold coins. Three Confederate soldiers, Baker (Livio Lorenzon), Stevens (Antonio Casas), and Jackson (Antonio Casale), know about the existence of the cashbox. The quest to possess the secret of its location and the box itself sets the three protagonists against each other in what will become a deadly struggle.

When the audience is introduced to each of the three gunmen, they are shown engaging in unethical and violent schemes for profit. They are all small-time criminals whose greed is stronger than their respect for life. Blondie and Tuco have a complex love-hate relationship, in which they systematically try to torture each other to death while being partners in a money-making scheme. Angel Eyes, who appears to have some earlier acquaintance with Blondie and Tuco, is a gun-for-hire who kills anyone for money.

One by one, they inadvertently learn of the secret. Angel Eyes learns of the gold first, when he is hired by Baker to find out from Stevens the name that Jackson is using as an alias. In the process, Angel Eyes kills Stevens and Baker, leaving Jackson as the only person alive who knows the location of the gold coins.

Blondie and Tuco encounter Jackson, who is using the name Bill Carson, as he is dying in the desert, the only surviving passenger of a Confederate stagecoach that was ambushed. Through Carson's dying words, Tuco learns that the gold coins are buried in a grave. He learns the name of the cemetery where the gold coins are buried but nothing more. Blondie, on the other hand, learns the name of the grave, but does not know the name of the cemetery. Blondie and Tuco, who have previously taken turns trying to kill each other, soon realize they must keep each other alive long enough to possess this prize, yet understand that there will be nothing to keep them from killing each other once it is found. It is this greed, codependency, and mutual distrust that propel their relationship throughout the unfolding narrative of the film, creating equilibrium that must be maintained through the film's climactic ending.

Blondie and Tuco eventually find the grave where the gold coins are buried, or so the audience is led to believe, but Angel Eyes, who has forced Tuco to divulge his half of the secret, is not far behind. Angel Eyes appears at the grave and the stage is set for the film's triadic confrontation between the three men. The three men soon become only two as Blondie kills Angel Eyes, leaving only himself and Tuco to share in the prize, truly "just like old times." The clever and manipulative Blondie then forces his old friend Tuco to put his head in a noose and to stand on a grave marker with his hands tied behind him. It appears, for a moment, that the two will now become one and that Blondie will be sole survivor of this quest for the fortune. In a final moment of goodness, Blondie spares Tuco's life through a gesture that is humorously reminiscent of their earlier money-making scheme, cutting the rope with a shot from his rifle. Blondie rides away with his half of the fortune and the film ends.

The relationship between the two surviving protagonists remains intact, denying the film the closure that might have resulted if only one survived. Good has triumphed over evil, but "good" and "evil" are only relative terms in the fictional world created by a Sergio Leone Western. Blondie, who displays many evil characteristics, is only relatively good; Tuco, who displays some good and many bad characteristics, may be no more ugly that the other protagonists; Angel Eyes, on the other hand, may in fact be completely bad, having no noticeable redeeming qualities whatsoever. The line that separates good and evil is blurred to the point that it no longer exists, or at least is indiscernible.

The similarity that exists between these three diverse characters is skillfully reflected in Morricone's music. As will be seen in chapter 5, goodness, badness, and ugliness are each represented by the same musical motif, but with its own distinguishing characteristics. This musical motif is the seed from which Morricone's score seems to organically grow.

The Film's Critical Reception

Would American audiences in 1967 respond to a low-budget Western starring a little-known television actor, much less an Italian-made Western? The answer would be "No," if they believed what Renata Adler wrote in her scathing review that appeared in the *The New York Times* in January 1968:

> "The Burn, the Gouge, and the Mangle" (its screen name is simply inappropriate) must be the most expensive, pious and repellent movie in the history of its peculiar genre. . . . The plot—and in their eagerness to mutilate someone, the writers continually lose track of it— seems to run as follows:
>
> A man whose pseudonym is Bill Carson, and who owns a clam-shaped snuffbox, knows the whereabouts of $200,000. Three characters, Burn (Clint Eastwood), Gouge (Lee Van Cleef) and the Mexican, Mangle (Eli Wallach)—whose names in the film are Joe, Setenza, and Tuco, respectively—are anxious to get a hold of it. . . . The action takes place in the West during the Civil War. That is all. It lasts two and a half slow hours.[4]

Adler was not the only critic who initially found the film long, slow-paced, and difficult to follow, even after United Artists shortened it by approximately fourteen minutes for its American release. As late as 1982, Brian Garfield wrote in *Western Films: A Complete Guide*:

> The impossible-to-follow plot has to do with rival thieves (all three stars) who keep double-crossing one another over stolen loot that is buried in a cemetery somewhere. . . . This was Leone's third Eastwood spaghettier and his longest movie before *Once Upon a Time in the West*; this one is more like a lasagner—a mashed-together deadweight mass of pasta, cheese and bloodsauce. . . . Like the *Dollars* movies this one is simpleminded and absurd; it's also long, slow and boring.[5]

In spite of such negative criticism, *The Good, the Bad and the Ugly* went on to become a commercial success due in part to the audiences' expectations of these Westerns, which were no doubt conditioned by the previous two Dollar films.

Other reviews, however, were a little more receptive and much less ignorant, such as the one Pat Broeske wrote for 1985's *Magill's Survey of Cinema*: "A morality play whose players have little morality—reflecting a common modern theme of a world-gone-mad in the face of war—*The Good, the Bad and the Ugly* weaves a stunning tapestry of vignettes both simple and sprawling."[6] It is perhaps the modern theme of the "world gone mad" and the American public's ability to relate to that theme in 1967 that may account for much of the film's domestic success.

The initial success and continued popularity of *The Good, the Bad and the Ugly* can be easily explained. Paul Smith elaborates:

> Sergio Leone's trilogy of so-called spaghetti Westerns . . . whatever their merits as movies, constitute an undoubtedly important and almost unique moment in the history of Hollywood cinema. Even though they were financed primarily by European capital, were shot in Italy's Cinecittà studios and on location in Spain, and used a mostly Italian work force, they have had a significant impact on the shape, style, and potentials of American movies ever since. Their importance is partly a function of the fact that they are the best-known instances of the production of what has been the only major and sustained revision of that central Hollywood movie genre, the Western, that has ever been undertaken outside Hollywood and largely without its capital.[7]

As surprising as this may have seemed to American audiences—an Italian film company copying a purely American genre and then successfully importing it into the United States—they responded positively at the box office.

America at War in the 1860s and 1960s

There are several factors that contributed to the increased box office success of *The Good, the Bad and the Ugly* when compared to its two predecessors. One factor was the increased budget for production and marketing due to United Artists' investment in the film. Another factor concerns the content of the film itself that contributed to the reception it had among American audiences in the 1960s. *The Good, the Bad and the Ugly* takes place during the American Civil War, which lasted from 1861 to 1865. In Leone's film, that particular war is depicted as extremely violent and completely senseless to all those involved, with the exception of some bureaucrats who are far removed from the actual conflict. In the 1960s, many Americans viewed the ongoing Vietnam War in precisely the same negative light, as a senseless conflict being perpetuated by politicians in Washington, D.C.

In fact, many Westerns of the 1960s were perceived as being dramatic expressions of political commentary on the Vietnam War or on war in general, whether they were intended to be or not. Historian John H. Lenihan describes this phenomenon:

> With President Johnson's escalation of the war in Vietnam, Westerns reflected the increasing skepticism and disillusionment with the direction of American foreign policy. Whereas Westerns of the fifties and early sixties idealized a frontier America struggling to substitute peaceful negotiation for a wasteful and unjust policy of military defeat, Westerns during the latter half of the sixties and early seventies conveyed a more critical and fatalistic view of a violence-prone nation that was contributing to prolonged and ultimately meaningless wars.[8]

Although *The Good, the Bad and the Ugly* is, for all practical purposes, an Italian film, its political commentary is as relevant to this discussion on American foreign policy of the 1960s as that of its Hollywood counterparts. Using one of the most violent periods in America's history as its canvas, *The Good, the Bad and the Ugly* paints a gloomy picture of war that Americans could easily comprehend. Lenihan continues:

> *The Good, the Bad and the Ugly* juxtaposes the unscrupulous conniving for money on the part of its hero (Clint Eastwood) against a background of civil war, where scores of men die for some remote cause. Near the end of the film, Eastwood's quest for the hidden loot is blocked by a raging battle for control of a strategic bridge. When Eastwood dynamites the bridge to stop the fighting and clear his path to the treasure, no one is more delighted than the dying Union com-

mander from whom (along with his troops) the long days of fighting have taken a tragic toll.[9]

During this battle, Eastwood's character, Blondie, offers his own political commentary on the war when he tells Tuco, "I've never seen so many men wasted so badly." Such an expression of distaste not only helps to define the character's apolitical personality, but is also an expression of Leone's antiwar sentiment. The fact that Blondie, who is Leone's personification of "the good," must overcome the presence of war as part of his quest for personal gain makes this film's comment on war clear: good is the antithesis of war and good must strive to overcome war just as it must strive to overcome evil. In this film, good eventually overcomes war so that his quest can continue, and soon thereafter defeats evil, "the bad," as well. Therein lies the appeal of Eastwood's character in this film as distinguished from the previous two Leone Westerns. To American audiences of the 1960s who had become accustomed to the images of real-life conflicts on the evening news, the escapism to an America one hundred years in the past, when one man can overcome the insanity of the war around him, must have been very appealing. The many Americans who felt that war was out of control would have found a hero who can manipulate war as he wishes to be very charismatic. That this hero, who exists outside of the military and the law, can accomplish his goals by quickly dispensing his own brand of justice only added to his charisma. Such charisma could have also influenced the collective consciousness of Americans, stimulating feelings of empowerment and a desire to exercise their rights to vote or publicly demonstrate in an effort to effect change.

American audiences had a sense of the hero's ability to overcome the difficulties of war before seeing the film. As they waited in line at the movie theater to see *The Good, the Bad and the Ugly*, they no doubt caught a glimpse of the movie poster with its tagline "For three men, the Civil War wasn't hell. It was practice!" The poster (frontispiece) shows the hero standing confidently and proudly alongside a cannon as he lights its fuse. The other two protagonists are standing nearby, holding their weapons and looking very threatening. All are pictured above the image of a violent Civil War battle as if they are somehow superior to it. In the film, all three protagonists manipulate the war to their advantage, demonstrating their superiority. Blondie and Tuco have the power to move a battle when it is in their way, and Angel Eyes is a sergeant in the Union Army, but he comes and goes and he pleases.

By contrast, the soldiers in both the Union and Confederate armies are portrayed in the film as pawns who are powerless to control their destinies. At one point, the Union captain tells a soldier, "It sure as hell might be you today, so go write your will." The captain's message is clear. Fate is inescapable. The similarity between these soldiers of the 1860s and American soldiers of the 1960s is obvious.

In *The Good, the Bad and the Ugly*, the similarity between soldiers of the 1860s and the 1960s can also be seen and heard in the cue "The Story of a Soldier" (figure 5.14), a solemn ballad about soldiers and their comrades who have made the supreme sacrifice. Although the English lyrics evoke images of the Civil War specifically, the message of the song would be equally as meaningful to audiences one hundred years later.

During World War II, many Hollywood films, melodramas in particular, were targeted at the young female demographic, women whose husbands were serving in the military. In the 1960s, when many wives were likewise left at home during the Vietnam War, it is surprising that a film so clearly targeted at a young male demographic would enjoy as much box office success as *The Good, the Bad and the Ugly*. This is not to say that women did not see this film; rather, it is significant that this film enjoyed the success it did in spite of the fact that many young men may not have had the opportunity to see it. The male audience at the time consisted of men too young or too old to serve in the military, men who had already served, men with military deferments for marriage or education, men who were medically ineligible, conscientious objectors, and draft dodgers.

Sergio Leone

Sergio Leone, director, cowriter of the story, and cowriter of the screenplay for *The Good, the Bad and the Ugly*, came from a show business family. He was born in Rome on 3 January 1929, the son of a silent-film director and an actress. He had relatively little experience as a film director before *A Fistful of Dollars*, having directed *Gli ultimi giorni di pompei (The Last Days of Pompeii)* in 1960, after its original director, Mario Bonnard, became ill. His first solo directorial effort was *Il colosso di rodi (The Colossus of Rhodes)* in 1961. *A Fistful of Dollars* (1964) was only his second solo effort. The commercial success of *A Fistful of Dollars* paved the way for Leone to create his second Western, *For a Few Dollars More* (1965). United Artists, who agreed to release Leone's first two Westerns in the United States, also helped to finance the production and marketing of Leone's third Western, *The Good, the Bad and the Ugly*.

Leone's research prior to the filming of *The Good, the Bad and the Ugly* was considerable. Not only did he study many Civil War photographs on which he based his cinematography, but he actually used genuine Civil War artillery in the film.[10] The visual effect is one of realism in film to which American audiences were not accustomed.

After *The Good, the Bad and the Ugly*, Leone went on to create two of his greatest works, *C'era una volta il west (Once Upon a Time in the West)* in 1968, starring Henry Fonda and Charles Bronson, and *C'era una volta in America (Once Upon a Time in America)* in 1984, starring Robert De Niro and James Woods. *Once Upon a Time in America* was the last film Leone directed before he died of a heart attack in 1989.

It is indeed noteworthy that all of the Leone films mentioned above include scores by Morricone. Leone and Morricone shared an artistically fruitful association, comparable to the director-composer association that existed between Sergei Eisenstein and Sergei Prokofiev (*Ivan the Terrible* and *Alexander Nevsky*), Alfred Hitchcock and Bernard Herrmann (*Vertigo, North by Northwest,* and *Psycho*), and Blake Edwards and Henry Mancini (*Peter Gunn, Breakfast at Tiffany's, The Pink Panther, 10, S.O.B.,* and *Victor/Victoria*). Such a prosperous association still exists between Steven Spielberg and John Williams (*Jaws, Close Encounters of the Third Kind, Raiders of the Lost Ark, E.T. the Extra-Terrestrial, Jurassic Park, Schindler's List,* and *Saving Private Ryan*). Of the twelve films directed by Leone during his career, eight are collaborations with Morricone, representing many of the most noteworthy contributions to film and film music by both men.

Clint Eastwood

After the release of *A Fistful of Dollars* and *For a Few Dollars More*, Clint Eastwood, who was born in San Francisco on 31 May 1930, had become a major box office draw and was seen as the heir apparent to the position held by John Wayne, that of the American hero as personified by the rugged frontiersman. The release of *The Good, the Bad and the Ugly* in December 1967 continued to enhance Eastwood's tough on-screen persona.

Clint Eastwood's first significant acting role was that of Rowdy Yates in television's *Rawhide*, which began in 1959. While on vacation from that show in 1964, Eastwood traveled to Italy to star in Sergio Leone's remake of Akira Kurosawa's *Yojimbo* (1961), which was titled *A Fistful of Dollars*, a story in which a drifter manipulates two rival families for his own profit. This was not the first time that a Western had been based on a Japanese film. Director John Sturges' *The Magnificent Seven* (1960) is a retelling of *The Seven Samurai* (1954), also directed by Kurosawa.

Leone had hoped to cast Charles Bronson or Henry Fonda in his first Western, but he finally settled on Clint Eastwood. Eastwood went on to reprise the role of "the man with no name" in two sequels, *For a Few Dollars More* in 1965 and *The Good, the Bad and the Ugly* in 1966. By the time the third film was released in the United States, audiences knew what to expect from a Clint Eastwood Western: lots of action, lots of gunfire, numerous dead bodies, and very little dialogue.

Eastwood's character in these three Westerns of Leone is a type of hero that must have seemed unfamiliar to many Americans at the time. Gone are the white hat, the white horse, and the clean-shaven wholesomeness that is normally associated with the stereotypical Hollywood Western hero. Eastwood's characters, with their unorthodox moral codes, help to redefine what qualities make up a Western hero. According to Dennis Bingham:

> Leone and Eastwood expose "good" as a subject construction built on codes of power and heroism familiar to the audience. They do this by showing just how far they can push the moral boundaries of "hero," while maintaining a viselike spectatorial identification with said "hero." By reducing heroism to ground zero—narcissism—Eastwood recuperates the myth of the subject in an era when ideals seem to have died.[11]

Eastwood's characters in these Westerns are powerful to the point of being omnipotent, manipulating families, towns, and armies, even though these characters must survive a brutal beating to prove it. These characters display an almost Christ-like ability to suffer a brutal beating at the hands of evil only to rise again triumphantly, as if the only reason for their resurrection is to cast judgment.

In *A Fistful of Dollars*, Eastwood's character is beaten up by the Rojos when his double-crossing is discovered. In *For a Few Dollars More*, Eastwood's and Lee Van Cleef's characters are beaten up by El Indio and his gang when they try to escape with the money from the Bank of El Paso. And in *The Good, the Bad and the Ugly*, Eastwood's character is tortured nearly to death by his vengeful partner Tuco. The spectator identifies with the hero, who eventually triumphs over his enemy. Good is victorious over evil, but good and evil are relative terms in the old American West of Sergio Leone.

In the United States, United Artists promoted Clint Eastwood's character as "the man with no name." To the contrary, in each of these three films, he is called by a (different) name. In *A Fistful of Dollars*, he's called "Joe" by the mortician. In *For a Few Dollars More*, he's referred to as "Monco" by a gentleman paying a bounty to Lee Van Cleef's character. In *The Good, the Bad and the Ugly*, his character, "the good" ("il buono"), is repeatedly called "Blondie" by Eli Wallach's character. However, the notes that accompany the Digital Video Disk (DVD) of *The Good, the Bad and the Ugly* list Clint Eastwood's character as Joe, the name his character was called in *A Fistful of Dollars*.[12]

Blondie, or Joe, is cool and confident; he can shoot through a hangman's noose with a single rifle shot. He smokes cigars, and when he kills, he rarely kills only one person at a time; three at a time is typical. The audience finds out he is from Illinois, but he shows no signs of loyalty toward the Union Army during the Civil War that is taking place around him.

These Westerns made Clint Eastwood an international star. After these Sergio Leone films he went on to star in several American-made Westerns, including director Don Siegel's *Two Mules for Sister Sara* (1970) and director John Sturges' *Joe Kidd* (1972). Eastwood directed and starred in *High Plains Drifter* (1973), *The Outlaw Josie Wales* (1976), *Pale Rider* (1985), and *Unforgiven* (1992), for which he earned an Academy Award as best director. The characters that he plays in these later Westerns share many of the qualities that made the "man with no name" a cultural icon, including his ability to express his own sense of right and wrong, usually through the use of a gun. Eastwood also starred as Inspector Harry Callahan in *Dirty Harry* (1971) and its four sequels, *Magnum Force* (1973), *The Enforcer* (1976), *Sudden Impact* (1983), and *The Dead Pool* (1988). Callahan is a twentieth-century

Blondie in many ways. He uses a gun to dispense his own brand of law enforcement based on a moral code that is often outside the law.

Eastwood ventured into other genres, with varying degrees of success, including the comedies *Every Which Way but Loose* (1978) and its sequel *Any Which Way You Can* (1980), and action films such as *Firefox* (1983), *In the Line of Fire* (1993), and *Space Cowboys* (2000). He directed and starred in the romance *The Bridges of Madison County* (1995) costarring Meryl Streep, a film in which his character bears little, if any, resemblance to Blondie.

A music lover all of his life, Eastwood can be seen playing piano in *In the Line of Fire*, which was directed by Wolfgang Petersen and features an effective and sophisticated, although not especially tuneful, score by Morricone. Eastwood recently began composing music for films, including *Mystic River* (2003), which he also directed. This score was a musical collaboration with veteran Hollywood composer and arranger Lennie Niehaus.[13]

Eli Wallach

Eli Wallach, who was born in Brooklyn,[14] is a graduate of the University of Texas at Austin, which is where he learned to ride a horse. He had been an actor on Broadway for some time when he made his 1956 film debut in *Baby Doll*. Before Sergio Leone's *The Good, the Bad and the Ugly*, Wallach's best-known role was that of Calvera, a Mexican bandit, in *The Magnificent Seven* (1960). About the filming of *The Magnificent Seven*, Wallach has humorously said that if he had heard Elmer Bernstein's music during filming, he "would have ridden the horse a little differently."[15] As will be seen in chapter 5, Wallach did in fact hear Morricone's music during the filming of one scene in *The Good, the Bad and the Ugly*.

Wallach's character, "the ugly" ("il brutto"), is a Mexican bandit named Tuco Benedicto Pacifico Juan Maria Ramirez, who often kills people and then performs the sign of the cross over their dead bodies. During the film, the audience learns that he has a long criminal record, several wives, and one brother, who is a priest. On a few occasions, Tuco appears to be illiterate, yet he makes fun of other people who cannot read. Like Eastwood's hero, Wallach's character exists outside the law and seems to have the power to manipulate the world around him.

Wallach went on to star in other films, but will most likely be best known for his performance as Tuco in *The Good, the Bad and the Ugly*. Wallach also enjoyed great success for his role as Don Altobello in *The Godfather, Part III* (1990).

Lee Van Cleef

Lee Van Cleef, who was born in Somerville, New Jersey, on 9 January 1925, had enjoyed some success in films before being cast in two of the Leone Westerns. His first film role was that of Jack Colby in *High Noon* (1952), an appearance that was followed by roles as villains in other lesser-known Westerns. Before being cast in *The Good, the Bad and the Ugly*, Van Cleef played the bounty hunter Colonel Douglas Mortimer, a retired army colonel seeking revenge for his sister's death, in Leone's *For a Few Dollars More*. It might seem odd to American audiences to see the same actor cast in different roles in two films that are supposedly part of the same trilogy. Leone had done that earlier when he cast Gian Maria Volonté as Ramón Rojo in *A Fistful of Dollars* and as El Indio in *For a Few Dollars More*. Volonté's character dies in each film. This would support the argument that these three Westerns of Leone are not actually a trilogy, due to contradictions in the audience's accumulation of knowledge of the characters played by Van Cleef and Volonté.

Van Cleef's character, "the bad" ("il cattivo"), is called Angel Eyes by everyone who knows him, but his name is actually Setenza.[16] The audience never hears him called this name in the film, at least not in the English-language prints. It is evident early in the film that he is a gun-for-hire, a freelance hit man who always sees his job through when he is paid. It is surprising to see him suddenly appear as a corrupt sergeant in the Union Army after Blondie and Tuco are captured wearing Confederate uniforms; when he reappears at the end of the film he is again out of uniform, ready for the climactic gunfight that ends the film.

After *The Good, the Bad and the Ugly*, Van Cleef starred in several lesser-known films playing a stereotypical villain. These include *Death Rides a Horse* (1968), *Sabata* (1970), and *The Return of Sabata* (1971). He enjoyed some success with the television series *The Master* in the mid-1980s. Like Leone, Van Cleef died of a heart attack in 1989.

Other Characterizations

Like their Hollywood counterparts, the lead characters in these three Leone Westerns are usually Caucasian Americans, played by either American or European actors. Other significant characters are Hispanic, as might be expected in the American Southwest, such as the Rojos and the Baxters in *A Fistful of Dollars*, or El Indio and his gang in *For a Few Dollars More*. However, these Hispanic characters are often played by Italian actors in Leone's films, which can be rather convincing, and rarely, if ever, are they played by Hispanic actors. In *The Good, the Bad and the Ugly*, Tuco is a good example of a Hispanic character played by a non-Hispanic actor, in this case, Eli Wallach, an American actor of Polish descent.[17]

Women occupy a very small space in the worlds created by Leone Westerns, at least those that predate *Once Upon a Time in the West* (1968). The only female character in *The Good, the Bad and the Ugly* who is significant enough to have a name is Maria, Bill Carson's girlfriend and a prostitute, who is a young Hispanic woman. Early in the film, the audience sees Stevens' wife, but never learns her name. Other females in this film are merely part of the scenery, such as elderly townspeople gathered to watch Tuco's hanging, a lady in a stagecoach talking with Angel Eyes, or an innkeeper's wife.

Hollywood Westerns of this time almost always featured a female lead character, usually as the love interest of a male lead character. In *The Good, the Bad and the Ugly*, there is no such love interest. In fact, as will be shown in chapter 5, the gold is given a feminine quality by Morricone's music, as if it is the beautiful woman after whom the three protagonists lust.

Native Americans are noticeably absent in all Leone Westerns. It seems odd that films that take place in the American Southwest of the nineteenth century would apparently avoid the presence of this culturally significant population. As Paul Smith observes:

> Indeed, there is an almost complete absence of Indians in the trilogy; symptomatically, the Hispanic character Tuco in *The Good, the Bad and the Ugly* is called upon to underscore this absence when, testing out guns in a store that he is about to rob, he fires at and destroys three wooden Indians, the only representations of Native Americans to appear in these movies.[18]

It is logical to conclude that since there are no Native American characters in these Leone Westerns, there would be no Native American actors either. It is possible that the lack of Native American characters is a result of the probable lack of appropriate acting talent in Europe, where these films were produced.

Masculinity

The Good, the Bad and Ugly is currently rated "R" in the United States, most likely for violence and language, but perhaps also for some brief nudity. In what is perhaps the only erotic moment in the film, Tuco is seen getting out of a bathtub and is completely naked except for the revolver he wears around his neck. He walks over to a closed hotel room door, expecting to surprise whoever is on the other side. Blondie, however, has surprised Tuco by entering the room through another door. He sees Tuco, and while talking to his naked friend, gently caresses the top of a bed post.

There is no heterosexual romance in this film, no love story and no tenderness, except possibly when Clint Eastwood's character is cleaning his pistol or when Eli Wallach's character is tenderly caressing the gold coins.

The only other hint of sexuality in this film is when Tuco, who has just been taken prisoner along with Blondie, confronts Corporal Wallace, who in turn punches Tuco in the stomach. Tuco replies, "I like big fat men like you." The joke is revealed and his fondness for men of that particular body type is clarified, however, in his next statement, "When they fall, they make more noise." Wallace eventually does fall, by Tuco's hand, and Tuco comments on the noise that the big man made.

Marcia Landy explains the complex male relationships that exist in the Westerns of Sergio Leone:

> Heterosexual romance in not a central motif and is subordinated to the motif of homosocial bonding. The relations between men—Mr. Mortimer and Monco in *For a Few Dollars More*, Cheyenne and Harmonica in *Once Upon a Time in the West*, Tuco and Blondie in *The Good, the Bad and the Ugly* (1966), and especially Juan and Sean in *Duck, You Sucker [A Fistful of Dynamite]*—are central and complex, involving a form of coupling that is ambivalent. The relations are based on economic competition but also on something else

that entails grudging admiration and respect, even if not affection and tenderness.[19]

It is perhaps this motif of "homosocial bonding," the love-hate relationships that exist between male characters who respect each other's strength while simultaneously competing against each other in life-or-death struggles for personal gain, that has earned these films their reputations as "guy films." Such films, usually centered on a man-against-man conflict, are typically marketed toward the male demographic.

The Good, the Bad and Ugly is indeed a "guy film." It is full of male egotism and masculine symbolism. There are plenty of unshaven faces complete with scars, blood, and sweat. Phallic symbols abound, such as the pistol that Blondie carefully cleans, the cigar that he occasionally shares with his partner Tuco, numerous rifles, and cannons. Even Morricone's music drips of masculinity at times, such as the magnificent mariachi-style trumpet solo at the film's climax as the three men compete against each other in a life-or-death battle for the prize.

The masculinity of each protagonist is highlighted by Leone's cinematography. When Eastwood's character first appears, attention is drawn to the gun belt he wears around his hips during the standoff with the three men attempting to apprehend Tuco. The framing of this male body's hips is reprised in the film's climactic standoff. Leone's montage includes close-ups of each man's gun belt as well as extreme close-ups of their eyes.

The Number Three

Throughout this film, there are numerous, and presumably intentional, appearances of the number three. This was the third of the three Westerns of Leone to feature Clint Eastwood, often referred to, somewhat inaccurately, as a trilogy. Several facts suggest that they are not a trilogy in the usual sense; Eastwood's character has a different name in each one, Van Cleef plays different characters in two of them, and Volonté's character dies twice.

There are three protagonists in this film. Each one is seen shooting three people before being given their epithet on screen. In the film's first scene, Tuco shoots the three men who try to ambush him in a ghost town. Later, Tuco shoots at three wooden Indians when testing a revolver, three shots to turn them sideways and three more shots to cut each one in half. Blondie almost always shoots three people at a time. When he first appears in the film, he shoots three men who are about to apprehend Tuco. Later, in a scene that was deleted for the American release, Tuco meets up with his three friends, Pedro, Chico, and Ramón. Blondie eventually shoots Tuco's three friends as they attempt to help Tuco recover reward money.

The secret of the gold coins is initially held by three men, Baker, Stevens, and Jackson. All three men eventually die and three other men, Blondie, Tuco, and Angel Eyes, take their places as bearers of the secret.

In another scene that was deleted for the American release, Blondie meets the other five members of Angel Eyes' gang. He counts each man, including Angel Eyes, and proclaims six as the perfect number. Angel Eyes, however, expresses his belief that three is actually the perfect number. Blondie replies by pointing out that he has six bullets in his gun.

The number three is most visually evident at the film's climax, as the three protagonists face off in a life-or-death contest for the prize, forming a triangle that is superimposed over the circular bed of stones in the center of a cemetery. Only one is killed, while the other two survive to share in the prize. Cumbow has observed: "As in *A Fistful of Dollars*, there is a tendency for the triangular opposition to resolve itself into two-and-one. Most often, of course, Blondie and Tuco are the two and Angeleyes [*sic*] is the one."[20] The fact that Blondie and Tuco are often "the two" is reinforced by the viewpoint, repeated by both characters throughout the film, that "there are two kinds of people in the world, my friend." In the end, however, the two eventually become one-and-one, as their relationship moves from one of codependence to one of independence once the gold coins are uncovered. Blondie rides off into the distance with his half of the loot and Tuco is left behind with one hundred thousand dollars and no horse, cursing his old friend and partner.

Deleted Scenes

Before *The Good, the Bad and the Ugly* was released in the United States, United Artists decided to make the film shorter. According to the notes that accompany the DVD that was released in the United

States in 1998, the film was approximately 175 minutes in length in its original Italian release. For its American release, the film was cut to 161 minutes. It is this version that appears on the American DVD.[21] The other fourteen minutes, because they were edited out before the film was dubbed in English, did not exist in English until recently. The version of the film that was released on DVD in Italy is 168 minutes, approximately seven minutes shorter than the original.

On 10 May 2003, the American Movie Classics cable channel broadcast an English-language version of the film with the missing fourteen minutes restored, including newly recorded dialogue from Clint Eastwood and Eli Wallach. All but one of these scenes are available in Italian as bonus tracks on the American DVD. They are similarly included as part of the feature film on the Italian DVD. However, there is one scene that is not on either DVD but was included in the American Movie Classics broadcast, a scene in which Tuco finds his three friends, Pedro, Chico, and Ramón, who are brothers and who later help him track down Blondie. These are the three men who unsuccessfully attempt to surprise Blondie at a hotel while he is cleaning his gun. This scene is approximately three minutes and eighteen seconds in length.

The inclusion of these deleted scenes has an impact on Morricone's score for *The Good, the Bad and the Ugly*. One of these scenes includes the first appearance of a musical cue. This is why the cues appear to be out of order on the soundtrack album when compared to the original English-language version of the film. When the missing scenes are taken into consideration, the cues on the soundtrack album are in the same order in which they occur in the film. As the film score is discussed in chapter 5, these scenes, and their musical cues, will be mentioned at the appropriate points in the film's narrative. In addition, there are numerous cues in the film that are not included on the original soundtrack album released by United Artists.

There are certain continuity issues that suggest that this film is best viewed in its most complete form, as the deleted scenes provide valuable information concerning several characters and events in the film. Additionally, to watch any Sergio Leone Western without its original letterbox formatting is to miss much of the director's intentions. This film must be viewed in its original widescreen version. Unfortunately, it is often televised in a reformatted version, and much of its cinematographic impact is lost.

The American DVD also includes as a bonus track the original American theatrical trailer. This trailer is significant because Angel Eyes' and Tuco's epithets, "the bad" and "the ugly," are reversed. Three times the trailer refers to Angel Eyes as "the ugly" and Tuco as "the bad," twice in the voice-over and once on screen. This error is most likely due to the fact that the original Italian title, *Il buono, il brutto, il cattivo*, does not translate as *The Good, the Bad and the Ugly*, but literally translates as *The Good, the Ugly (and) the Bad*. One needs to merely consult an Italian/English dictionary to discover this dreadfully conspicuous error.

4

THE MUSIC AND ITS CONTEXT

Before discussing each cue from *The Good, the Bad and the Ugly*, as shall be done in the next chapter, it is helpful to place this film score stylistically among Morricone's other cinematic works. Many of his film scoring techniques were discussed in chapter 2. Chapter 3 presented the film from the perspective of the media and movie audiences of the time. This chapter will focus on Morricone's score for *The Good, the Bad and the Ugly* as it compares to his other film scores, particularly those immediately preceding this film.

By the time Ennio Morricone composed the music for *The Good, the Bad and the Ugly* in 1966, he had already composed music for numerous Italian films, some of which were mentioned in chapter 1. Italian audiences were familiar with his distinctive sound, an eclectic texture that combines instruments, both acoustic and electric, and voices, both as carriers of words and as instruments. American audiences, however, would not hear his music in a theater until the following year.

The Music's Critical Reception

Morricone had already completed the score to the third Dollar film, *The Good, the Bad and the Ugly*, by the time the first two Leone Westerns were released in the United States, so he was almost certainly unfamiliar with his music's critical reception in this country until long after the release of the third film in Italy. Nevertheless, when *The Good, the Bad and the Ugly* was finally released in the United States on 29 December 1967, American moviegoers probably had become familiar with Morricone's music. Unfortunately, the American media failed to embrace this new style of Western and its music, their musical palettes no doubt being dulled by the more conventional and predictable images and sounds of Hollywood Westerns.

A Fistful of Dollars

The first Leone Western, *A Fistful of Dollars*, was released in the United States on 18 January 1967. Morricone's unique orchestration is unmistakable from the beginning to the end of this film score. The "Main Title," for example, includes many of his trademarks, such as the human whistle; the acoustic and electric guitars; exotic percussion, including the whip, the anvil, and the bell; and the soprano recorder. As mentioned in chapter 2, Morricone uses a theme based on the D minor hexatonic scale in the "Main Title" as he does for the "Main Title" of *The Good, the Bad and the Ugly*. Another Morricone trademark is the mariachi-style trumpet solo that is reserved for the film's climax, the final confrontation between good and evil.

Morricone's choice of these unusual instruments, as unconventional as they may seem when compared to the instruments heard in Hollywood scores, was deliberate and well thought out. As Morricone explained his approach to Miceli:

> It has always been my belief that one of the most important creative tools of a film composer is timbre. I began to first think this way when carefully examining the scenes and the protagonist in *A Fistful of Dollars*, and then, later on, in all the other Leone films. Westerns have helped mold my thinking, at least those envisioned by Leone, as picaresque, playful, dramatic, amusing, bittersweet, and over the top.[1]

Morricone's skillful command of his musical timbres in *A Fistful of Dollars* is certainly one of the most distinguishing characteristics of that film score. Morricone's music for other Leone Westerns, in addition to its obviously dramatic character, is often playful and amusing, such as his quotation of Mozart's *Eine kleine Nachtmusik* in *Giù la testa* (1971).

Unfortunately, the same qualities that distinguish Morricone's music from many Hollywood composers are the same qualities that film critics of the time disparaged. Bosley Crowther of *The New York Times* said about Leone's film and Morricone's music, "Filmed in hard, somber color and paced to a musical score that betrays tricks and themes that sound derivative (remember "Ghost Riders in the Sky"?), *A Fistful of Dollars* is a Western that its sanguine distributors suggest may be loosing a new non-hero on us—a new James Bond. God forbid!"[2] To describe Morricone's score for this film as consisting of tricks that are somehow derivative borders on absurdity. The reference to "Ghost Riders in the Sky" may have some validity, as discussed in chapter 2, with that song's representation of the "electric cowboy" through the use of electric guitar in country and western music and its subsequent crossover into rock-and-roll. Morricone featured the electric guitar in *A Fistful of Dollars*, of course. To ask for divine intervention to prevent the distributors from releasing a new non-hero, the so-called man with no name, as United Artists had marketed Clint Eastwood's character, is humorous, as Crowther no doubt intended it to be. United Artists was planning to do just that, in hopes of duplicating the success that they were enjoying importing the James Bond films from England. They had released the commercially successful *Thunderball*, the fourth James Bond film starring Sean Connery, on 29 December 1965, slightly more than a year before their release of *A Fistful of Dollars*.

For a Few Dollars More

On 10 May 1967, only four months after United Artists' American release of *A Fistful of Dollars* and slightly more than one month before their release of *You Only Live Twice*, the fifth James Bond film, they released *For a Few Dollars More* in the United States. Morricone's style in this score is unmistakable as he once again features the human whistle, the electric guitar, and the climactic mariachi-style trumpet solo.

Reviewers were equally as harsh as they had been when critiquing the first Leone Western. Crowther again includes references to Morricone's score in his *New York Times* review: "In the close-up faces of his ugly ruffians, highlighted and shadowed in burnished hues, and in the ominous thump of drums and wail of trumpets that preface his menace scenes, he [Leone] prepares us for the violent explosions that mark the deadly circuit of pursuit."[3] Morricone's music does indeed preface much of the action in these Westerns, demonstrating his ability to cleverly create the appropriate mood—suspense, fear, danger—as a musical prelude to the dramatic action on the screen. As mentioned in chapter 2, the trumpet, wailing or not, is Morricone's first choice for the most climactic moments in a Western. An anonymous reviewer for *Time* magazine likewise comments on Morricone's *For a Few Dollars More* score: "For those who like an elemental Western with galvanic gestures, a twangy score full of jew's-harps and choral chanting, and a lofty disdain for sense and authenticity, the film will be ideal."[4] It is difficult to know if the reviewer is commenting positively or not by describing the score as "twangy." In fact, this score is perhaps Morricone's most twangy Western score. Morricone features the jew's harp and his trademark wordless vocals in this score as well. That the reviewer mentions these qualities along with "lofty disdain for sense and authenticity" suggests that the reader should take these comments in a negative light. Joseph Morgenstern of *Newsweek* magazine, in his review cleverly entitled "The Via Veneto Kid," also makes note of Morricone's unusual orchestration: "As in Chinese opera, ritual noises punctuate emotions: one theme is a frivolous six-note figure played on an ocarina, another is a more somber one-note solo on a jew's harp."[5] The ocarina, a mainly spherical wind instrument made of clay or porcelain and played like a flute, will be discussed in chapter 5 as it has an important presence in *The Good, the Bad and the Ugly*.

The Good, the Bad and the Ugly

Film critics such as Crowther and Morgenstern may lament Morricone's use of unconventional instruments, no doubt being accustomed to the more comfortable and familiar sounds of a Hollywood film score for this particular genre, but it is often Morricone's orchestration that sets his scores apart from his Hollywood counterparts, perhaps more than any other characteristic. As Cumbow explains:

> Much of what is astounding about Morricone's scores for Leone derives from the composer's eccentric approach to the orchestration. His association of a whistling voice with a wandering loner (in the five Westerns) is the most melodic of a library of devices he uses to create a non-orchestral music: The *sproing!* of the jew's harp, the *wah-wah* of an amplified harmonica, also whipcracks, gunshots, and the exotic arsenal of less identifiable twangs, bangs, clicks, and clangs, characterize his orchestration of the savage.[6]

Indeed, Morricone had astounded some critics with his scores for Sergio Leone's first two Westerns, while provoking hostility from others. In the score for *The Good, the Bad and the Ugly*, he took his innovative orchestration style one step further, more deeply exploring the many possibilities of the human voice. It is worth mentioning, however, that the jew's harp, which nearly every American critic singled out in the second Leone Western, is noticeably absent in his score for *The Good, the Bad and the Ugly*.

When *The Good, the Bad and the Ugly* was finally released in the United States, Morricone's music still met with surprisingly mediocre reviews from film critics in the American media. *Variety* magazine said that "Ennio Morricone's insistent music and Carlo Simi's baroque art direction further contribute to the pic's too-muchness."[7] One is left to interpret exactly what "too-muchness" means, but it no doubt refers to the brilliant foreground presence of Morricone's music. According to the *Rolling Stone Record Guide*, Morricone's music for *The Good, the Bad and the Ugly* was the "least exciting of Morricone's Leone scores."[8] And Garfield actually describes the music as "Ennio Morricone's unusually lifeless score."[9] In spite of the cool reception by film and music critics, the soundtrack recording of *The Good, the Bad and the Ugly* became a best-seller in the United States, due in part to radio airplay being given to a cover version of the "Main Title" by Hugo Montenegro.

Once Upon a Time in the West

After *The Good, the Bad and the Ugly*, Sergio Leone and Ennio Morricone collaborated on several other successful films, including the Westerns *C'era una volta il West* (1968, released as *Once Upon a Time in the West* in the United States in 1969) and *Giù la testa* (1971, released as *A Fistful of Dynamite*, a.k.a. *Duck, You Sucker*, in the United States in 1972).

There are several factors that distinguish *Once Upon a Time in the West* from Leone and Morricone's earlier collaborations on Westerns. Most noticeable is the fact that this film has a female as one of the main characters (played by Claudia Cardinale). Also, it is the first Western of Leone that did not star Clint Eastwood. In this film, three men (played by Henry Fonda, Charles Bronson, and Jason Robards) are more concerned with the woman and her land than with money. Morricone's score for *Once Upon a Time in the West* is likewise distinguished from his earlier Westerns in that, unlike the three Dollar films, the main theme of this film is in D major, not D minor. This change of mode helps to further separate this film from the previous Leone Westerns.

Once Upon a Time in the West represents the next step in the evolution of Morricone's style as well as Leone's. It is a longer film than *The Good, the Bad and the Ugly* by more than thirty minutes (in their original versions). Leone's cinematic style is unmistakable, consisting of panoramic landscapes, moving camera, point-of-view shots, and extreme close-ups juxtaposed with extreme long shots. Morricone's style, although similarly unmistakable, shows signs of his continued experimentation. His use of the voice is more conservative, employing the beautiful wordless soprano, but without the male voice as heard in the coyote yell or wah-wah sound of *The Good, the Bad and the Ugly*. His experimentation here mainly involves musique concrète. The "Main Title" sequence consists of mechanical and natural sounds, such as a squeaky waterwheel, the tapping of a telegraph, the dripping of water, the buzzing of a fly, and the sound of the approaching train. In *For a Few Dollars More* and *The Good, the Bad and the Ugly*, natural or mechanical sounds are cleverly incorporated into the music. By contrast, in *Once Upon a Time in the West*, these sounds are accompanied by no other musical sounds. In effect, these very rhythmic sounds become the music.

Orchestration

No discussion of Morricone's score for *The Good, the Bad and the Ugly* would be complete without dedicating time to the human whistling, wordless vocals, soprano recorder, bass ocarina, orchestral chimes, acoustic guitar, electric guitar, mariachi trumpet, military bugles, and diverse percussion that make up Morricone's distinctive score for this film. Morricone skillfully blends acoustic instruments, such as the classical guitar, soprano recorder, English horn, trumpet, and string orchestra with electric instruments, including the guitar and organ. Other sounds are best described as musique concrète. As Morricone told Sweeting:

> I come from a background of experimental music which mingled real sounds together with musical sounds . . . so I used real sounds partly to give a kind of nostalgia that the film had to convey. I also used

these realistic sounds in a psychological way. With *The Good, the Bad and the Ugly*, I used animal sounds—as you say, the coyote sound—so the sound of the animal became the main theme of the movie. I don't know how I had this idea. It's just according to your experiences, and following the musical avant-garde.[10]

This animal sound, which will be discussed in chapter 5, represents one of the three protagonists in *The Good, the Bad and the Ugly*. Other non-musical sounds that are evident in the music of this film are the sounds of crows, church bells, cannon fire, and gunshots, sounds which can be considered diegetic. These sounds, many of which help to define the physical space of the film, have a profound effect on the score, whether they were conceived as part of the music or not. The listener, however, may not know the difference between those sounds conceived musically and those conceived as part of the film's diegesis.

Morricone's skillful use of the electric guitar and his distinct preference for the minor-sounding modes, Dorian in particular, in his Western scores were discussed in chapter 2. These characteristics are clearly evident throughout his score for *The Good, the Bad and the Ugly*, as will be seen in the next chapter. Tagg describes in detail this unique gift that Morricone demonstrates for blending timbres from such a wide variety of musical genres into his own unique sound:

Between 1958 and 1964 Morricone derived most of his income from arranging and conducting popular music (*musica leggera*), activities in which the electric guitar was an accepted part of the ensemble. His use of the instrument for the Italian Western was therefore standard procedure and never intended as a novelty. Morricone also emphasizes that his use of modality in Western films was in no way an attempt at sounding Anglo-American instead of Italian or European but rather part and parcel of his own musical style, whether he be writing for film, pop singers or the concert hall. Like any professional composer working in the media, Morricone had to be completely and competently eclectic. Therefore, having to arrange the minor-modal Woody Guthrie ballad *Pastures of Plenty* for US-American singer Peter Tevis in 1962 was no extraordinary task. What distinguished Morricone from contemporaries composing and arranging such music for popular media purposes was, however, his ability to combine current idioms of popular composition with those of the avant-garde without making the end result sound pretentious.[11]

Much more will be said about Morricone's use of the electric guitar in the "Main Title" of *The Good, the Bad and the Ugly* in chapter 5. However, it is now sufficient to say that these compositional techniques, which were perceived as novelties by American film critics in the mid-1960s, had become part of the popular music scene in Europe when Morricone was composing his first Western film scores.

Soundtrack Album

United Artists Records, part of the same company that released Leone's Westerns in the United States, released the soundtrack album to *The Good, the Bad and the Ugly* (LP) in 1966, a year before the film's domestic release. That recording was eventually on the *Billboard Magazine Top Ten* list. The same album was later released on Compact Disc by EMI-Manhattan Records, a division of Capitol Records, in 1985. In order to make these recordings more commercially appealing, record companies released them in versions that were slightly different from those heard in the film. Many of the sound effects, such as animal sounds, gunshots, and cannon fire, which are heard during the music in the film, have been left out of these recordings. Also, some editing was done to make the cues shorter, perhaps to make them more appealing for radio airplay. In addition, the tracks on the soundtrack album appear to be out of order because of the absence of the first appearance of the cue "The Strong" in the shorter English-language prints of the film. This is not true of the original Italian version of the film, which is approximately fourteen minutes longer.

In 2001, the *Complete Original Motion Picture Soundtrack* for this film was released on Compact Disc by GDM Music. This recording includes many of the cues that were excluded from the original United Artists Records album. In most of the cases where cues were edited for the United Artists Records album, the longer, unedited versions are included on the GDM recording. The GDM Compact Disc also includes a very attractive package that lists the performers on the recording as well as all four verses of the song "The Story of a Soldier."

The impact of the soundtrack album on the audience should not be underestimated. To Morricone, it is extremely important for the soundtrack album to be released on Compact Disc. As he explained to Burlingame and Crowdus of *Cineaste* in 1995, this is because sometimes the director finds it necessary to hold back the music and so it cannot really make the contribution it would have wanted to make. In that sense, a Compact Disc is a way for the composer to vindicate himself, to revalidate his music. The Compact Disc enables the audience to finally hear the music they couldn't hear during the film.[12]

Morricone is making a very powerful statement concerning the existence of a film score as an entity completely separate from the film itself. This remarkable declaration implies that film music can exist on the same level as concert music, but this is not absolutely true. Some film music, however, has been rearranged for concert performances, including Morricone's. Morricone is actually saying that soundtrack recordings can help the educated listener to better appreciate the contribution of the film composer to the viewing experience. Although it is unlikely that any of Morricone's music could not be heard during *The Good, the Bad and the Ugly*, familiarity with the soundtrack album can certainly enhance the viewing of that film. The situation Morricone describes, that of film music being "held back," applies to some of his later scores, a good example of which is his music for Wolfgang Petersen's *In the Line of Fire* (1993), starring Clint Eastwood.

A few words should be said about the titles of the tracks on the soundtrack album, as they appear in English along with their original Italian titles. "Marcetta" would be better translated as "Short March," not as "Marcia," which is simply Italian for "March." On the Compact Disc, "Marcetta Senza Speranza" is translated as "Marcia without Hop," which is confusing. Not only would "Marcetta" be better as "Short March," but "Hop" should be "Hope," a typographical error that appears on both the back cover of the Compact Disc package and the CD itself. However, a reproduction of the back cover of the original LP appears on the back of the Compact Disc package, with the correct spelling. This makes the best translations of "Marcetta Senza Speranza" as "Short March without Hope" or possibly "Short Hopeless March."

In chapter 5, the musical cues of the film will be discussed in the order in which they occur in the film. It is in the spirit of a guide or roadmap through the score that this discussion will take place. It is hoped that the reader will understand and appreciate the cleverness that Morricone demonstrates throughout this film and the significance of each of the musical cues as they relate to the film's unfolding narrative. There are musical signifiers in many of these cues, such as the military bugle calls to represent the armies, the soprano voice that feminizes the gold coins, and the sound of the coyote to highlight Tuco's untamed personality.

Many of the musical cues in this film are quite short, often consisting of no more than one or two motives from the "Main Title." This can be considered one of Morricone's stylistic traits that distinguish his scores from those of his contemporaries—the ability to combine short motives or "cells" to form brief but informative cues. In spite of the fact that many cues in this film are unusually short, every effort has been made to include all of the film's cues in the following discussion, no matter how short or insignificant each may appear to be at first.

5

ANALYSIS OF THE SCORE

The collaborations of Sergio Leone and Ennio Morricone include many of the most sophisticated contributions to the Western genre. Morricone's score for *The Good, the Bad and the Ugly* is representative of his most innovative work for that genre. This is not to imply that his other Western scores are less significant, but rather that an appreciation of all of his Western scores can be developed by an understanding of the complex musical structures that are found in his score for this particular film.

The music's place in the narrative construction of this film often serves to inform the viewer in ways that the image and dialogue do not. This is due to Leone's practice of involving Morricone in the creation of the film very early in production and to Morricone's belief that music must say what the dialogue and image do not. Leone viewed music as something so integral to the film's production that he would often ask for Morricone's music to be composed and recorded in advance, and played back during filming. Leone employed this uncommon practice in the Westerns *The Good, the Bad and the Ugly* and *Once Upon a Time in the West* and in the gangster film *Once Upon a Time in America*. To accomplish this, the director and composer must work closely to develop the cinematic concept behind each musical cue.

Analytical Methodology

An analysis of Morricone's music for *The Good, the Bad and the Ugly* will provide answers to the question "Why does this music sound unmistakably Morriconian?" These answers can be found in many musi-

cal components of each cue. One is a matter of tonality: his use of the
minor modes and the pentatonic and hexatonic scales that make up
many of his themes. His use of tonality often includes harmonizations
that are indicative of the Dorian mode. Another is his use of modern
elements: the occasional incorporation of minimalism or musique concrète. Yet another is his easily recognizable style of orchestration that
diverges from the classic Hollywood scores of his contemporaries. Still
others include the brevity with which he can provide the viewer with
information about the film's characters and events, and the foreground
presence that his music has in the context of a Leone Western.

As Morricone's music is so tightly interwoven into the unfolding
fabric of this film's narrative, a chronological approach to these musical cues is most appropriate. In the following discussion of the cues that
make up his score for *The Good, the Bad and the Ugly*, it is hoped that
the many facets of Morricone's contributions to the art of film music,
and to the Western genre in particular, will be made evident. The
names of these cues come from the commercially available soundtrack
album Compact Discs with some strategic amendments by the author
for clarity.[1]

"Main Title"

Many Hollywood scores begin and end featuring a standard symphony
orchestra and add other, more descriptive instruments throughout the
film only as needed, saving the full arsenal of instrumental tone colors
for the most climactic moments in the film. Morricone, on the other
hand, wastes no time in displaying his huge arsenal of magnificent
sounds and tone colors, beginning with the "Main Title" sequence of
The Good, the Bad and the Ugly, thus leaving very little to the listener's imagination. But as he so often does, he finds other ways to
surprise the audience throughout the film, not just with his unusual
combinations of different tone colors, but with fast and exciting minor-
key themes; slow, mournful, and sometimes soaring major-key themes;
dramatic shifts in tempo; gradual Beethoven-like crescendos of musical
energy; and occasionally an abrupt halt so he can begin to build the
level of excitement all over again. The "Main Title" of this film show-
cases many of the extraordinary tone colors that make this score so
outstanding.

The first five notes of the "Main Title," which shall be referred to as Motive 1A, are without a doubt the nucleus of this entire film score, often occurring as a musical cue by themselves or in conjunction with Motive 2A. The "Main Title" begins with an exposition of Motive 1A heard three times, each time performed on a different instrument or voice representing each of the film's three protagonists in the order in which their epithets appear in the film's Italian title, "il buono" ("the good"), "il brutto" ("the ugly"), and "il cattivo" ("the bad").

Miceli describes these three very distinct sounds as the "flautto diritto soprano"[2] (soprano recorder), representing Blondie or "the good"; "due voci virili, trattate elettronicamente"[3] (two male voices treated electronically), a scream that Morricone describes as the sound of a "coyote,"[4] performed an octave lower, representing Tuco or "the ugly"; and finally, an "ocarina bassa"[5] (bass ocarina), playing two octaves lower than the original, representing Angel Eyes or "the bad."[6] These three distinct tone colors, the soprano recorder, the coyote, and the bass ocarina, will be used by Morricone throughout the film to signify each of the three protagonists. He will use them to inform the audience which protagonist is performing or about to perform some dramatic action.

The exposition of these three distinct timbres for Motive 1A is followed by two measures of drum beats on a tom-tom, which is perhaps the only allusion in this score to the music of Native America. The very recognizable and memorable theme of the "Main Title" (figure 5.1)[7] begins in the third measure.

The first time measures three through ten are heard (the A section of the musical form), Motives 1A and 1B are played on the soprano recorder, signifying "the good," and Motives 2A, 2B, 2C, and 2D are given a distinctive wah-wah sound, which, according to Morricone, is a human voice.[8] Miceli describes this distinctive sound as "una voce virile molto meno trattata—il timbro è metallico, tagliente—che ne pone in evidenza il carattere canzonatorio"[9] (a male voice modified very little—with a metallic and sharp timbre—that has a flippant character about it). This sound has a metallic timbre that is reminiscent of the harmonica or the trumpet with a harmon mute. Morricone will use this very unusual sound throughout the score, often when Motives 1A and 2A occur together as a complete musical cue.

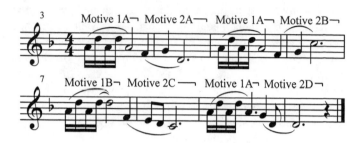

Figure 5.1: "Main Title," A Section
from *The Good, the Bad and the Ugly* by Ennio Morricone
© 1966, 1968 (Renewed) Edizioni Eureka (Italy)
Rights for the world outside Italy controlled by U.S. Music International, Inc.
Rights in the U.S.A. and Canada administered by EMI Unart Catalog Inc. (Publishing)
and Warner Bros. Publications Inc. (Print)
All Rights Reserved. Used by Permission.
WARNER BROS. PUBLICATIONS U.S. INC., Miami, FL 33014

This sudden transition from one motive of this theme to the next is the best evidence in this score of Morricone's micro-cell technique, the immediate juxtaposition of short and often contrasting musical ideas (in the form of trichords, tetrachords, pentachords, and hexachords) in a process resembling serialism. As mentioned in chapter 1, Morricone has acknowledged the use of his micro-cell technique in this film score, but the application of the technique as part of his compositional process remains a mystery. The results of this technique, however, can be seen in the A section of the "Main Title." Here, motives consisting of three, four, and five notes, with very contrasting timbres and melodic contours, are cleverly combined to form one very cohesive and recognizable theme.

In addition to the motives shown in figure 5.1, the sounds of gunshots are added to the A section of the "Main Title."[10] Measures three through ten are then repeated, but this time the soprano recorder is replaced with the bass ocarina, signifying "the bad," and the wah-wah sound is replaced by the human whistle, a timbre that was quite prevalent in Morricone's music for the first two Leone Westerns.

The A section of the musical form appears to be in the key of D minor, a key that Morricone used throughout the previous two Leone Westerns and will use throughout this score as well. The melody of this section, as mentioned in chapter 2, is based on a minor hexatonic scale that is derived from Aeolian or Dorian, excluding the sixth scale degree. When the theme is harmonized later, it is done so using D minor, G major, and C major triads, indicating that Morricone is actually using the Dorian mode. He has described this theme as being based on a scale from D to D with no sharps or flats, a scale that includes B-natural and not B-flat.[11] After measures three through ten are repeated, there is a very brief transition after which Morricone abruptly presents the B section of the form, beginning with a pick-up note before measure twelve and featuring an electric guitar solo reminiscent of the instrumental rock-and-roll groups of the early 1960s (figure 5.2). As will be seen, the melody of the B section also includes many B-naturals.

Figure 5.2: "Main Title," B Section
from *The Good, the Bad and the Ugly* by Ennio Morricone
© 1966, 1968 (Renewed) Edizioni Eureka (Italy)
Rights for the world outside Italy controlled by U.S. Music International, Inc.
Rights in the U.S.A. and Canada administered by EMI Unart Catalog Inc. (Publishing)
and Warner Bros. Publications Inc. (Print)
All Rights Reserved. Used by Permission.
WARNER BROS. PUBLICATIONS U.S. INC., Miami, FL 33014

The brilliant sound of the electric guitar is in sharp contrast to the tone colors just heard in the A section. The electric guitar solo is accompanied by a wordless male chorus, which adds an accompanying rhythmic figure at first, but then fills in the harmony with long sustained chords. This melody cadences on C, followed by C-sharp, the leading tone in the key of D minor, as preparation for the return of the A section. Morricone will occasionally introduce the leading tone of a minor key in preparation for a repeat of the minor-key theme, as he does here.

Much has already been said about Morricone's use of the brilliant-sounding electric guitar and that instrument's place in the culture of the modern American West, as opposed to the old American West. It should also be mentioned that the B section of the "Main Title" is, with one small exception, the only place Morricone uses this instrument in this film (it also is used for Motive 2A when following Motive 1A played on the bass ocarina). Morricone will, however, reprise the B section of the "Main Title" in subsequent musical cues several times in the film. When he does so, this music always signifies forward motion by one or more of the protagonists in the film, either on foot, on horseback, or in a stagecoach. Its syncopated rhythm is what Tagg refers to as a "horse rhythm,"[12] a rhythmic device that film composers often employ in music for Westerns because it seems reminiscent of the galloping of a horse's hooves.

After the B section, which ends in measure twenty-seven, there is a reprise of the A section, but this time it features the coyote sound for Motives 1A and 1B, signifying "the ugly," and the wah-wah sound returns for Motives 2A, 2B, 2C, and 2D. This return to the A section is followed by new music that includes military-like bugle calls, representative of the Civil War era in which the story takes place, performed ad libitum and accompanied by sustained chords from a mixed chorus and orchestra. After a short transition featuring Motive 1A with the sounds of the coyote and soprano recorder respectively, the B section of the form returns, followed by an abbreviated reprise of the A section—including the soprano recorder alternating with the coyote sound for Motive 1A and the wah-wah sound for Motives 2A and 2B—which ends the complex and informative "Main Title."

Following the "Main Title," there is a long and suspenseful scene in which three men are seen slowly approaching a saloon in what appears to be a ghost town. The three men enter the saloon, gunshots are heard, and Tuco, who has apparently just shot the three men, crashes through the front window of the saloon. The action freezes as the audience hears the coyote version of Motive 1A and the wah-wah version of Motive 2A, and Tuco is given his epithet, "the ugly," on the screen.[13] As Jeff Smith points out, "As each title appears, there is a freeze frame under which the main musical motive plays as a kind of leitmotiv. However, rather than distinguishing each character by a separate theme à la Wagner, Morricone distinguishes Blondie, Angel Eyes, and Tuco through different orchestrations of the *same* leitmotiv."[14] Morricone's approach to the use of the leitmotif was discussed in chapter 2. Tuco has just shot, and presumably killed, three gunmen, one of whom reappears in the film seeking revenge for this shooting. Tuco then jumps on a horse and rides away.

"The Sundown"

The next musical cue is "The Sundown," and it is heard as Angel Eyes rides on horseback toward a farmhouse as the sun is about to set. It is played slowly and with much *rubato* on the acoustic guitar,[15] giving this cue a southwestern American character. It begins with a beautiful cadenza-like melody (figure 5.3) and is in the key of D minor.

As he often does in his music for Westerns, Morricone demonstrates a distinct preference for the natural form of the minor scale, in which the seventh scale degree, C-natural, is not raised. The southwestern American flavor of this cue is comparable to the mariachi trumpet solos that Morricone uses during the climactic conflicts of the Dollar films. Played on instruments associated with the traditional music of the American Southwest, these themes derive their lyrical quality from their melodic contour, which is mainly conjunct (stepwise). After this guitar melody, Angel Eyes' Motive 1A is heard, played on the bass ocarina, before the acoustic guitar reenters with a more suspenseful tune consisting of perfect fourths, A to D and D to G, played on the open strings of the guitar. Morricone will occasionally use the open strings of the guitar, demonstrating a preference for the quartal harmony that is implied. This tune is heard as Angel Eyes dismounts from his horse and walks into the farmhouse. Although the acoustic guitar will return for other cues, "The Sundown" is a cue that is only heard once in this film.

Figure 5.3: "The Sundown"

What follows is another long and suspenseful scene with no music
or dialogue as Angel Eyes enters the house, slowly walks down a hallway from the entrance to the dining area, sits down at a dinner table
with the man who lives there, and begins to eat. The audience finds out
later that this man is named Stevens. Angel Eyes has been hired by a
man named Baker to get information from Stevens. Angel Eyes gets the
information he wants—the alias under which a man named Jackson is
living—and also learns of the missing gold coins. Stevens, afraid that
Angel Eyes has been sent to kill him, offers Angel Eyes money in
hopes that he will spare his life. Unfortunately, Angel Eyes interprets
this gesture as a counteroffer for killing Baker instead. Stevens, fearing
for his life, nervously reaches for his gun, but Angel Eyes shoots him
from under the table, killing him. After he shoots Stevens, the audience
hears a high string tremolo as the tension builds and Angel Eyes also

shoots Stevens' oldest son, who has appeared from upstairs. Morricone will often use the sound of a high violin tremolo to create tension in a scene, either as a prelude to a dramatic event, such as when Clint Eastwood's character is about to shoot and kill four of the Baxters' men in *A Fistful of Dollars*; during an event, as he does during the cue "Setenza" later in this film; or after an event, such as he does here.

The audience then hears Angel Eyes' Motive 1A, played on a bass ocarina, followed by Motive 2A played on an electric guitar (the only use of this instrument other than the B section of the "Main Title") as the scene changes to Baker's home. Angel Eyes talks with Baker about Stevens and the information that Stevens gave him. Angel Eyes tells Baker that Stevens also gave him money, presumably to carry out a killing in return. Angel Eyes begins to suffocate Baker under a pillow, then shoots through the pillow and kills him. There is a short solo from the English horn and, as the action freezes, Angel Eyes is given his epithet on the screen, "the bad." The audience then hears Motive 1A on the bass ocarina and Motive 2A on the electric guitar played once more. Like Tuco, Angel Eyes has now shot and presumably killed three people.

When the audience is first introduced to Blondie, he is not seen but his voice is heard as he interrupts three men who are about to take Tuco captive in order to collect a reward of two thousand dollars. Blondie shoots and kills the three men and the audience hears a vocal version of Motive 1A and the wah-wah version of Motive 2A. Like Tuco and Angel Eyes, Blondie has now killed three men, but he is not yet given his epithet on the screen. Moments later, Blondie begins a conversation with Tuco about the reward being offered for his capture. This scene is followed by one in which Blondie turns in Tuco to a town sheriff and collects reward money. Moments later, Tuco is shown sitting on a horse with a noose around his neck as he is about to be hanged. Blondie's presence in a nearby livery stable is made known by the sight of cigar smoke coming around the edge of a second-story window and, as the smoke is seen, his Motive 1A and the wah-wah version of Motive 2A are heard. Blondie then appears, Motives 1A and 2A are heard again, and as Tuco is about to hang, Blondie shoots through the hangman's noose freeing Tuco, who rides away on horseback. Blondie and Tuco meet in the desert later to divide the reward money in half. Tuco asks for more than half of the reward money in the future, but Blondie cleverly tells him, after offering him a cigar, that lowering his percentage might "interfere with my aim."

Blondie and Tuco are seen repeating the scam in another town. Angel Eyes is nearby asking an old soldier, who is a double amputee, questions about Baker, Stevens, Jackson, and the missing money. After Angel Eyes pays the old soldier for the information, he boards a stagecoach and sees Blondie waiting to shoot through Tuco's noose. Angel Eyes, who is talking to a lady in the stagecoach, refers to Blondie as a "golden-haired angel" who is watching over Tuco. The audience hears a very short music cue that sounds like a heavenly chorus of angels as Blondie sits on his horse.

The hanging continues, Blondie shoots, but this time it takes three shots to cut the rope. After the first two shots, the horse on which Tuco was seated rides away. Tuco hangs from the rope for a moment until the third shot cuts him free. Tuco runs away from the center of town along with Blondie, who is still on horseback. Tuco is seen jumping onto the horse behind Blondie. As Blondie and Tuco ride away from town, the audience hears the B section of the "Main Title," featuring the electric guitar solo. Morricone will often use the B section for traveling music as Blondie and Tuco are in motion.

After Blondie and Tuco venture out of town, the two argue. Tuco complains that "when that rope starts to pull tight, you can feel the devil bite your ass." Blondie, obviously frustrated with Tuco's complaining, decides to abandon him in the desert. As Blondie is about to ride off, he stops, turns to Tuco, and says, "Such ingratitude, after all the times I've saved your life." The action freezes and he is finally given his epithet, "the good." His Motive 1A and the wah-wah version of Motive 2A are heard again. The A section of the "Main Title" continues with the soprano recorder and human whistle as Blondie rides away. Then, as Tuco is cursing Blondie, Tuco's Motive 1A and the wah-wah version of Motive 2A are heard and the scene ends.

"Setenza"

The next scene includes one of the few examples of diegetic music in this film, music whose source exists in the world created by the film's narrative. A group of men are heard singing as they ride in a horse-drawn wagon with a woman. They push her out of the wagon and continue on their way. The woman is Maria, Jackson's girlfriend, and Angel Eyes is waiting for her inside her home to find out where Jackson, who is using the alias Bill Carson, is hiding. As he begins beating her for information, the short musical cue "Setenza" is heard. The cue begins with an English horn solo followed by Motive 1A played on the bass ocarina and Motive 2A on the electric guitar, signifying Angel Eyes. Motive 1A is heard again, this time on the English horn, which Morricone uses to represent several minor characters in the film, and is followed by a high sustained tremolo in the violins as Angel Eyes continues to beat her. The music suddenly stops as she finally gives in to his interrogation. She tells him that Bill Carson is with General Sibley and the Third Cavalry, but she does not know their destination. Angel Eyes will continue his search for Carson, the only person still alive who knows the location of the gold coins.

"The Rope Bridge"

Next, a scene occurs that includes a short music cue as Tuco, whom Blondie abandoned in the desert, is seen crossing a rope bridge on his way to a small town where he eventually steals a gun and robs the gun shop owner. This cue includes a four-note ostinato (figure 5.4), played on the acoustic guitar, an ostinato that Morricone will use in several cues throughout the film, occasionally on the acoustic guitar, but more often on the piano.

Figure 5.4: "The Rope Bridge," Four-Note Ostinato in D Minor
from *The Good, the Bad and the Ugly* by Ennio Morricone
© 1966, 1968 (Renewed) Edizioni Eureka (Italy)
Rights for the world outside Italy controlled by U.S. Music International, Inc.
Rights in the U.S.A. and Canada administered by EMI Unart Catalog Inc. (Publishing)
and Warner Bros. Publications Inc. (Print)
All Rights Reserved. Used by Permission.
WARNER BROS. PUBLICATIONS U.S. INC., Miami, FL 33014

The ostinatos in this cue are quite reminiscent of the minimalist music of the middle and late twentieth century, in which the repetition of a short musical idea is the basis for the music's formal structure. This ostinato consists of a D minor triad with an added appoggiatura. D minor, the key of the "Main Title" and "The Sundown," is a key to which Morricone will often refer throughout this score.[16]

Just before Tuco finds Blondie, who is now at a hotel cleaning his gun, three of Tuco's friends, named Pedro, Chico, and Ramón, try to surprise and kill Blondie. Morricone will use a string tremolo once again to accentuate the impending danger. Blondie senses the danger, loads his gun, and kills Tuco's three friends in yet another recurrence of the number three in this film. Blondie's Motive 1A and the wah-wah version of Motive 2A are heard once more. Tuco appears in the window and, while holding Blondie at gunpoint, forces him to stand on a wooden stool and put his neck in a noose. But before Tuco can hang Blondie by shooting the legs from the stool, a cannonball blasts through the hotel and Blondie escapes. The sight of the empty noose is accompanied by Blondie's Motive 1A and the wah-wah version of Motive 2A.[17]

"The Pursuit"

As Tuco is seen on horseback searching for Blondie, Morricone uses the A section of the "Main Title" to accompany the scene. At first, he uses Blondie's Motives 1A and 1B and the human whistle for the other motives. The theme is repeated with Tuco's Motives 1A and 1B and the wah-wah sound replacing the whistle. Morricone then uses the B section of the "Main Title" as the scene continues. As he often does, he uses the B section while one or more of the protagonists, usually Blondie and Tuco, are in motion. The A section is heard again, including Tuco's coyote sound and the wah-wah sound alternating with the soprano recorder and human whistle. This clever intertwining of Tuco's and Blondie's timbres coincides perfectly with Tuco's discovery of Blondie's cigar at an abandoned campsite. The B section returns again, followed finally by a short English horn solo and Tuco's Motive 1A with the wah-wah version of Motive 2A. The English solo horn returns as the scene changes, and Blondie's Motive 1A and the human whistle Motive 2A are heard once more.

Tuco finds Blondie, who is now engaged in the reward-money scam with a new partner named Thomas "Shorty" Larson. Tuco interrupts Shorty's rescue by Blondie, and Shorty dies. Tuco then leads Blondie into the desert at gunpoint to torture him as he seeks revenge for the time Blondie abandoned him in the desert. The cue "The Desert" is heard as Tuco and Blondie make their way across the hot, dry sand.

"The Desert"

"The Desert" is a reflection of Morricone's twentieth-century influences and is representative of his modernist contribution to film music. The cue begins with a long and suspenseful introduction featuring a tonally ambiguous and disjunct piano melody accompanied by sustained string tremolos. After this introduction, Morricone gives the audience a beautiful English horn[18] melody (figure 5.5).

Figure 5.5: "The Desert," English Horn Solo
from *The Good, the Bad and the Ugly* by Ennio Morricone
© 1966, 1968 (Renewed) Edizioni Eureka (Italy)
Rights for the world outside Italy controlled by U.S. Music International, Inc.
Rights in the U.S.A. and Canada administered by EMI Unart Catalog Inc. (Publishing)
and Warner Bros. Publications Inc. (Print)
All Rights Reserved. Used by Permission.
WARNER BROS. PUBLICATIONS U.S. INC., Miami, FL 33014

This theme bears a great resemblance to a twelve-tone row, as both phrases that make up this melody contain eleven different pitch classes.

The only pitch class missing is G-sharp. This melody is surprisingly tonal and appears to be in the key of A minor, suggesting that the missing pitch class is the *leading tone*, a note that no classical composer would ever hesitate to use. This not only demonstrates Morricone's preference for the natural form of the minor scale, but is evidence of his desire to avoid the harmonic form of the scale, which is much more common in tonal music, even in such a tonally ambiguous cue. As Jeff Smith explains, "the piece is characterized by a high degree of tonal instability and chromaticism and is the most musically ambitious piece in the entire score."[19]

When the English horn arrives at the sustained A3 in measures five through eight and the A4 on the repeat, it is accompanied by a four-note piano ostinato (figure 5.6), similar to the acoustic guitar ostinato in "The Rope Bridge." The presence of the ostinato serves to reinforce the key of A minor. This eerie melody is heard as Blondie is forced to walk across the hot sand without water. He is shown with blisters on his face as he collapses from exhaustion.[20] Blondie is near death and the tonal ambiguity of the cue seems to highlight his dreadfully ambiguous future.

Figure 5.6: "The Desert," Four-Note Ostinato in A Minor
from *The Good, the Bad and the Ugly* by Ennio Morricone
© 1966, 1968 (Renewed) Edizioni Eureka (Italy)
Rights for the world outside Italy controlled by U.S. Music International, Inc.
Rights in the U.S.A. and Canada administered by EMI Unart Catalog Inc. (Publishing)
and Warner Bros. Publications Inc. (Print)
All Rights Reserved. Used by Permission.
WARNER BROS. PUBLICATIONS U.S. INC., Miami, FL 33014

After this theme, the piano ostinato is heard again, followed by a three-note orchestral ostinato (figure 5.7)[21] that Morricone uses with two different note values (eighth notes and sixteenth notes) simultaneously, creating an effect known as *hemiola*. As this cue ends, Tuco prepares to shoot Blondie in the head, but his plans are interrupted by the appearance of an approaching stagecoach being pulled across the desert by a team of six horses with nobody at the reins.

Figure 5.7: "The Desert," Three-Note Ostinato in E Minor
from *The Good, the Bad and the Ugly* by Ennio Morricone
© 1966, 1968 (Renewed) Edizioni Eureka (Italy)
Rights for the world outside Italy controlled by U.S. Music International, Inc.
Rights in the U.S.A. and Canada administered by EMI Unart Catalog Inc. (Publishing)
and Warner Bros. Publications Inc. (Print)
All Rights Reserved. Used by Permission.
WARNER BROS. PUBLICATIONS U.S. INC., Miami, FL 33014

"The Carriage of the Spirits"

As the stagecoach is seen approaching from the distance, Morricone gives the audience what is, in many ways, one of the most complex and informative music cues in the film. "The Carriage of the Spirits" consists mainly of a trumpet melody in B-flat major (figure 5.8), or possibly G minor, a melody that Morricone also uses in a cue titled "The Strong." This melody uses the notes of a B-flat pentatonic scale (B-flat, C, D, F, G), or, if one considers the key to be G minor, uses five of the six notes of a G minor hexatonic scale (G, B-flat, C, D, F), a transposition of the scale that Morricone used in the "Main Title." This majestic melody is used to signify fallen soldiers.

Morricone's music provides the audience with a wealth of information about the stagecoach. The trumpet melody signifies the fallen soldiers in the stagecoach; bugle calls are heard representing the military to which these soldiers belong; and a beautiful countermelody, featuring a wordless soprano vocal high above the trumpet, adds a feminine quality to the cue. One of the dying soldiers inside the stagecoach, Bill Carson, knows the secret of the gold coins. Morricone is using the soprano voice to feminize the gold coins as if they are things of beauty after which the protagonists will lust. The soprano will be heard again, near the end of the film, as Tuco searches for the grave where the gold coins are buried.

Figure 5.8: "The Carriage of the Spirits" ("The Strong")
from *The Good, the Bad and the Ugly* by Ennio Morricone
© 1966, 1968 (Renewed) Edizioni Eureka (Italy)
Rights for the world outside Italy controlled by U.S. Music International, Inc.
Rights in the U.S.A. and Canada administered by EMI Unart Catalog Inc. (Publishing)
and Warner Bros. Publications Inc. (Print)
All Rights Reserved. Used by Permission.
WARNER BROS. PUBLICATIONS U.S. INC., Miami, FL 33014

Tuco soon learns that the stagecoach contains the bodies of dead and dying Confederate soldiers. The side of the stagecoach says "3rd Regt.," but Bill Carson, one of the soldiers inside, was said to be with the Third Cavalry, a possible continuity error. Tuco is surprised to find Carson still alive inside the stagecoach. Carson offers Tuco two hundred thousand dollars in gold coins in exchange for water. Tuco interrogates Carson to find out the location of the gold coins. Before giving Carson any water, Tuco learns that the coins are buried in a grave at Sad Hill Cemetery, but Carson does not tell him which grave. It becomes apparent that Carson may not survive without water. Tuco runs to his horse to get water, but as he returns, he discovers that Blondie has somehow made his way to the stagecoach and, in Carson's dying words, has learned the name of the grave.

Tuco realizes that he must now keep Blondie alive, as he is the only person who now knows the name of the grave where the gold coins are buried, and the audience hears the A section of the "Main Title" featuring the soprano recorder (Blondie's Motives 1A and 1B) and the wah-wah version of the other motives. Blondie and Tuco's relationship has now changed from one of friendship and hate, in which they try to kill each other even though they are friends and business partners, to one of codependency, in which neither one can possess the prize without the other one's help.[22]

"Mission San Antonio"

Tuco takes Blondie to Mission San Antonio, a Catholic mission in Texas, at which Tuco's brother, Pablo (Luigi Pistilli, who also appeared in *For a Few Dollars More*), is a priest. As Blondie and Tuco enter the mission, with the help of another priest, they see many injured soldiers and the audience hears the cue "Mission San Antonio," which is an instrumental version of the cue "The Story of a Soldier" and features a beautiful horn solo in D major ("The Story of a Soldier," in its complete vocal form, will be discussed later). Moments later, the audience hears a shorter version of this melody featuring the oboe. This cue soon segues to a new theme, also in D major, that features the flute, oboe, and English horn (figure 5.9).

Figure 5.9: "Mission San Antonio"
from *The Good, the Bad and the Ugly* by Ennio Morricone
© 1966, 1968 (Renewed) Edizioni Eureka (Italy)
Rights for the world outside Italy controlled by U.S. Music International, Inc.
Rights in the U.S.A. and Canada administered by EMI Unart Catalog Inc. (Publishing)
and Warner Bros. Publications Inc. (Print)
All Rights Reserved. Used by Permission.
WARNER BROS. PUBLICATIONS U.S. INC., Miami, FL 33014

The cue ends with Motive 1A played on the English horn and the wah-wah version of Motive 2A as Tuco eagerly waits to learn if Blondie will survive.

After Blondie begins recuperating at the mission, Tuco visits him and cunningly tries to find out the name of the grave. While trying to convince Blondie to divulge his half of the secret, Tuco, trying to endear himself to Blondie, asks Blondie about his family. Tuco tries to bond with Blondie by dishonestly proclaiming that, like him, he also has no family and is all alone in the world. The tension is humorously broken when Blondie throws coffee in Tuco's face and Blondie's Motive 1A and the wah-wah version of Motive 2A are heard again.

"Tuco's Brother"

After Blondie regains his health, Tuco visits him again. An older priest enters the room and tells Tuco that Father Ramirez has just returned to the mission. Ironically, it becomes apparent that Tuco has family and that Father Ramirez is in fact Tuco's brother. There is a short music cue that features a beautiful acoustic guitar solo as Tuco visits with his brother who has just returned from their father's funeral (figure 5.10).

Figure 5.10: "Tuco's Brother"
from *The Good, the Bad and the Ugly* by Ennio Morricone
© 1966, 1968 (Renewed) Edizioni Eureka (Italy)
Rights for the world outside Italy controlled by U.S. Music International, Inc.
Rights in the U.S.A. and Canada administered by EMI Unart Catalog Inc. (Publishing)
and Warner Bros. Publications Inc. (Print)
All Rights Reserved. Used by Permission.
WARNER BROS. PUBLICATIONS U.S. INC., Miami, FL 33014

Tuco and his brother, Pablo, talk about their parents. Tuco learns that their mother has been dead for several years and that their father just recently passed away. Pablo appears disappointed in his brother and acts as if he is not pleased to see him. As Blondie eavesdrops on them, the two men talk about the different paths that they have chosen for their lives and Tuco accuses his brother of being a coward. The two brothers end up arguing, eventually striking each other, and the guitar solo is heard a second time. After the visit, Blondie and Tuco leave the mission in the Confederate stagecoach, and Tuco, who had earlier claimed to be all alone in the world, brags about what a great brother he has. The audience hears the acoustic guitar solo a third time, followed by the B section of the "Main Title" which is here used as traveling music once more.[23]

"Short March"

Blondie and Tuco, who are wearing Confederate uniforms, encounter Union Army troops, but they mistake them for Confederate troops at first. Once they realize that the soldiers' dusty uniforms are blue and not gray, the audience hears Tuco's Motive 1A and the wah-wah version of Motive 2A. This humorous error quickly places them in a Union prison camp. As Blondie, Tuco, and the other prisoners are seen marching into the camp, Morricone gives the audience a "Marcetta" or "Short March" (figure 5.11). He features two of his favorite sounds to evoke the character of the old West, the harmonica, which begins the melody, and the human whistle, which is added in measure thirteen. The sound of the harmonica and whistle appears to be diegetic, but the audience does not see a harmonica or the prisoners' faces as they whistle. Once Blondie and Tuco and the other prisoners are inside the walls of the camp, a large man named Corporal Wallace (Mario Brega, who also appeared in *A Fistful of Dollars* and *For a Few Dollars More*) is seen conducting roll call of the new prisoners.

The march is in the key of D major, the parallel major key of D minor, which is the key of the "Main Title" and "The Sundown." Morricone will use the keys of D major and D minor throughout the film, but surprisingly, the fast and exciting music is often in the minor key while much of this film's slow and sad music is in the major key. This atypical use of major and minor keys can be considered one way in which Morricone breaks with a well-established musical convention.

Figure 5.11: "Short March"
from *The Good, the Bad and the Ugly* by Ennio Morricone
© 1966, 1968 (Renewed) Edizioni Eureka (Italy)
Rights for the world outside Italy controlled by U.S. Music International, Inc.
Rights in the U.S.A. and Canada administered by EMI Unart Catalog Inc. (Publishing)
and Warner Bros. Publications Inc. (Print)
All Rights Reserved. Used by Permission.
WARNER BROS. PUBLICATIONS U.S. INC., Miami, FL 33014

A slower version of the march is heard as the scene changes to the interior of the captain's quarters. The captain is watching roll call through a telescope. His attention soon becomes focused on Angel Eyes. Angel Eyes, who is now a Union Army sergeant, hears roll being taken and is caught off guard when he hears "Bill Carson," Jackson's alias, called out by Corporal Wallace. Tuco claims to be Carson, and Angel Eyes becomes determined to find out if Tuco now knows what Carson knew—the location of the gold coins. This cue ends as another soldier arrives and summons Angel Eyes to the captain's quarters.

The captain and Angel Eyes discuss the treatment of their prisoners. The captain tells Angel Eyes that he knows of thieves who are bivouacked near the camp, dealing in goods stolen from the prisoners. He accuses Angel Eyes of mistreating, beating, and killing prisoners. The captain is dying of gangrene and swears to bring to a court-martial all those who dishonor the Union Army uniform. Angel Eyes sarcastically wishes him luck and leaves. During this confrontation, bugle calls are heard from elsewhere in the camp. It was most likely Morricone who carefully and cleverly chose these historically accurate bugle calls to be used throughout the film. The call heard in this scene is *Assembly* (figure 5.12), which signals that soldiers are to "fall in."

Figure 5.12: *Assembly*

Another instrumental version of the cue "The Story of a Soldier" is then heard as the scene changes to an exterior view of the prison camp. Angel Eyes is then seen dealing with the thieves who are selling the prisoners' valuables.

A few moments later, Angel Eyes asks Corporal Wallace to bring him Tuco, who is now using Jackson's alias, Bill Carson. Angel Eyes invites Tuco into his office and they begin to eat and drink together. Angel Eyes begins to question Tuco about where he was captured and why he's using the name Bill Carson. During the questioning, another bugle call is heard from somewhere within the camp. This bugle call is *Drill* (figure 5.13), which signals it is time for soldiers to march or to practice using weapons.

Figure 5.13: *Drill*

As mentioned in chapter 2, these bugle calls can be perceived as being diegetic, since it is logical to assume they come from a source that exists in the world created by the film's narrative, even though no bugler is ever seen in the film.

The military bugle is a member of the trumpet family, but, unlike a modern trumpet, it has no valves. As such, it is limited to the pitches of the harmonic series. Since bugle calls rarely ascend above the sixth harmonic, bugle calls are consequently triadic. In other words, bugle calls consist of the notes of a major triad; in the case of all of the bugle calls heard in *The Good, the Bad and the Ugly*, this triad is B-flat major. It should be mentioned that Morricone's recurring four-note ostinatos (figures 5.4, 5.6, and 5.17) are also triadic. By contrast, many of his ostinatos, with the exception of some of those heard in "The Trio" (figure 5.20), consist of the notes of a minor triad with an added appoggiatura. This major and minor duality helps to distinguish the film's protagonists from the war that surrounds them and highlights their existence outside the military and political system.

"The Story of a Soldier"

As Angel Eyes and Tuco continue dining together, Angel Eyes stands up, walks over to a window, and gives a signal for music to begin. A band of musician prisoners begins to play and sing "The Story of a Soldier" (figure 5.14).[24] The audience sees the musicians outside playing violins, flutes, harmonicas, a valve trombone, a bass drum, a guitar, and an accordion. Inside his office, Angel Eyes asks why Tuco has Bill Carson's tobacco box. Angel Eyes closes the box on Tuco's fingers and cuffs him to the wooden chair in which he is sitting. Wallace suddenly appears and begins torturing Tuco, as Angel Eyes continues questioning him about Bill Carson and what Carson told him about the gold coins.

"The Story of a Soldier" is a touching ballad in honor of soldiers who die for their fellow man. The English-language lyrics are by songwriter Tommie Connor. In addition to the four different verses shown here, there is a fifteen-measure instrumental interlude after verse four.[25] During this interlude, one of the prisoners, who is playing a violin, becomes so overcome with grief that he can no longer play. He puts down his violin bow and the guard in charge shouts, "Play that fiddle, you!" The prisoner begins playing again, but the sound of his single violin is enhanced to sound more like a string orchestra. After the interlude, verse five is sung again.

Morricone will use this theme throughout the film to signify the suffering of soldiers, both Union and Confederate. Its sentimental tone is in stark contrast to the brutal torture that is seen going on inside Angel Eyes' office. The scene alternates between Wallace's beating of Tuco and the musicians outside, who know that they are there only to cover up the sound of Tuco's cries for help. With the exception of the song the men were singing as they threw Maria from their wagon, this is the only cue in this film score for which Morricone uses the human voice with words. There is a very logical and practical reason why he does so here. The voices heard are diegetic; they are the voices of people who are known to exist in the world created by the film's narrative. Morricone often uses the human voice without words, but the people to whom those voices belong are not characters in the story; those voices are instruments in the nondiegetic music of the film. Like the "Short March," "The Story of a Soldier" is in the key of D major. This is another example of Morricone defying the musical convention of using minor keys for sad, sentimental music and major keys for brighter, more joyous music. However, he writes so skillfully in either setting that he is able to evoke the desired emotion in spite of his unusual choices of key.

Figure 5.14: "The Story of a Soldier"
from *The Good, the Bad and the Ugly* by Ennio Morricone
"The Story of a Soldier," by Ennio Morricone and Tommie Connor
© 1966, 1968 (Renewed) Edizioni Eureka (Italy)

"The Story of a Soldier" is significant for another reason. Many authors have discussed Leone's practice of occasionally asking the composer to write music before a scene is filmed so that the music can be played on loudspeakers as the filming takes place. According to Brown, "Morricone's music was played throughout the shooting of *Once Upon a Time in the West*, supplying its rhythms and affects to actors and technicians alike. For other films, certain sequences were built around the music."[26] Without a doubt, one of those other films was *The Good, the Bad and the Ugly*. When asked if any of the music for *The Good, the Bad and the Ugly* was composed before the film was made, Morricone replied, "I seem to recall that for *The Good, the Bad and the Ugly*, I did not write much music before the actual filming took place. One thing is certain, however. I did write the chorus, before filming, for the scene in which they were to place fingers in Tuco's eyes."[27] He is referring to Wallace's beating of Tuco in Angel Eyes' office, during which Wallace presses his thumbs into Tuco's eyes. Tuco, unable to endure any more pain, finally tells Angel Eyes his half of the secret. According to Eli Wallach (Tuco), this music cue, "The Story of a Soldier," was in fact being played over loudspeakers as the scene was being filmed.[28]

Wallace's beating of Tuco finally ends as Tuco tells Angel Eyes that the gold coins are buried in a grave at Sad Hill Cemetery. Tuco explains that only Blondie knows the name on the grave. Angel Eyes plans to become Blondie's new partner. Angel Eyes has Blondie brought to his office. Blondie enters, speaks with Angel Eyes about the money, and sees Tuco's blood on the office floor. As Blondie pauses to reflect on Tuco's beating, not knowing if his old friend has survived, the eight-measure instrumental introduction from "The Story of a Soldier" is heard again.

"The Military Train"

Wallace then takes Tuco to the train station to join other prisoners on their way to execution or incarceration. As Wallace and Tuco, who are handcuffed to each other, make their way toward the train, the audience hears the cue "The Military Train," which is the same theme that Morricone used in "Short March," but it is slow and played on a solo harmonica, an instrument Morricone often chooses for serious, somber moments in his Western scores, as in the graveyard scene in *A Fistful of Dollars*. After Wallace and Tuco board the train, the harmonica version of this cue is heard again and the train departs the station.[29]

Some time after the train leaves the station with Tuco and Wallace on board, Tuco pretends to need to urinate. Tuco and Wallace stand by the open door of the box car in which they are traveling. Tuco jumps off the train, taking Wallace with him. He kills Wallace and attempts to remove the handcuffs from his wrist. Morricone once again uses "The Story of a Soldier," this time to accompany Wallace's death, perhaps as a signifier of his suffering or as a reminder of Wallace's earlier torture of Tuco. After the eight-measure instrumental introduction, the first half of verse one (measures one through eight) is heard. However, unlike the previous time this theme was heard, the audience is forced to recognize the voices that are singing as nondiegetic, as there are no prisoners or anyone else in the scene who could possibly be singing this song. The presence of these nondiegetic voices with words is somewhat unsettling, as the audience expects them to have a source within the story, unlike Morricone's use of the voice without words.

Unable to free himself from Wallace's dead body, Tuco places Wallace on the train tracks and waits for the next train. A train eventually passes by, severing the handcuffs under its wheels and violently mutilating Wallace's dead body in the process. Tuco quickly jumps on board the train and escapes. As he jumps onto the last car of the train, the audience hears Tuco's Motive 1A and the wah-wah version of Motive 2A.

"The Death of a Thief"

In the next scene, which takes place in a town through which the Union Army is traveling, Blondie is seen riding with Angel Eyes, who is no longer in uniform, and his gang. The audience hears the A section of the "Main Title" featuring Blondie's Motives 1A and 1B the wah-wah version of the other motives. Soon thereafter, a prisoner, wearing a sign around his neck that says in part "thief," is shown being executed by a firing squad, and Morricone then uses the cue "The Strong," which includes the trumpet melody previously heard in "The Carriage of the Spirits," to signify the soldier's death. Later in the film, Morricone will once again use this majestic trumpet melody to signify the death of a soldier.

"The One-Armed Gunman"

Tuco suddenly appears, trying not to be noticed in the crowd of soldiers and civilians in the street. He enters an abandoned hotel, finds a hotel room with a bathtub full of water, and takes a bath. One of the three gunmen thought to have been killed by Tuco in the first scene of the film reappears with his right arm missing. Morricone uses a short and suspenseful musical cue that begins with Motive 1A on the English horn, an instrument that represents no single character in particular, as the gunman recognizes Tuco and decides to follow him. The one-armed gunman follows Tuco into the hotel room and finds him in the bathtub. As he is about to shoot Tuco, with a gun in his left hand, he stops and talks to Tuco about spending the last eight months looking for him while learning to shoot a gun left-handed. Tuco, who is hiding his gun under the bathwater, shoots him several times and he falls to the floor. Tuco stands up and gets out of the bathtub, shoots again and says to the dying man, "When you have to shoot, shoot, don't talk!"

The scene changes to one of Blondie, who is inside a bombed-out building with Angel Eyes and his gang, as the audience hears Blondie's Motive 1A and the wah-wah version of Motive 2A. He apparently has heard Tuco's gunshots and says, in a piece of dialogue that may actually be a prediction about the music Morricone would later compose to represent each of the film's three protagonists, "Every gun makes its own tune." In this film score, every gun (Blondie, Tuco, and Angel Eyes) does indeed make its own tune, as signified by Morricone's orchestration of Motive 1A.

Blondie makes his way to the hotel as Morricone uses a slower version of the A section of the "Main Title" to accompany him, featuring Blondie's Motives 1A and 1B with the wah-wah version of the other motives. This is followed by a repeat of the A section that includes Angel Eyes' Motives 1A and 1B and a flute for the other motives, as Angel Eyes sends one of his gang after Blondie. Blondie shoots and kills the man following him. These two versions of the A section are heard again as Blondie finds Tuco, who is naked and standing inside the hotel room.

"Two against Five"

Blondie and Tuco reunite, and Tuco plans to seek revenge on Angel Eyes before continuing in the search for the gold coins. The cue "Two against Five" begins with a suspenseful introduction, featuring timpani and various other percussion instruments, as Angel Eyes and his surviving gang members discover the body of the man who was following Blondie. Angel Eyes and his gang decide to go in search of Blondie and Tuco. The cue continues with Motive 2A on the cello as Blondie offers to go with Tuco in search of Angel Eyes.

As Blondie and Tuco walk together through the center of town, the cue continues with the B section of the "Main Title," which Morricone once again uses as traveling music. This is followed by more suspenseful music featuring mostly percussion. One by one, Blondie and Tuco kill all of the men in Angel Eyes' gang, but Angel Eyes, who has left a note saying "See you soon, idiots," flees.

An abbreviated version of the B section of the "Main Title" is heard again as Blondie and Tuco continue their trek toward the cemetery where the gold coins are buried. Tuco appears to have a map that he has been using to help him find Sad Hill Cemetery.[30] They soon find themselves surrounded by Union Army soldiers and are escorted to the captain in charge (Aldo Giuffrè). These troops are engaged in a battle for a bridge over a river. The captain, who is obviously an alcoholic, thinks the battle is absurd and only has value because his superiors say that it does.

The next musical cue heard is "The Strong" (figure 5.8), as Blondie and Tuco are led to see the captain. Morricone used this cue earlier in the film to signify a soldier's death. It appears here as a signifier of the captain's impending fate. Blondie and Tuco pretend that they want to enlist.[31] As Blondie, Tuco, and the captain march through the troops waiting for battle, the audience hears the "Short March" played slowly on a harmonica. Blondie and Tuco learn that the captain secretly wishes to blow up the bridge.

The Confederate Army begins its attack and the captain is told that the troops are awaiting his orders. After the captain stops one soldier from prematurely firing his weapon, two bugle calls are heard. The first is *Attention* (figure 5.15), a signal for all soldiers to be at attention, often played before another call is sounded.

Figure 5.15: *Attention*

The second call, which is heard after all of the companies report that they are ready, is *Commence Firing* (figure 5.16), a signal for all soldiers to begin firing their weapons. Like the bugle calls heard earlier in the film, no bugler is seen, only assumed to be present.

Figure 5.16: *Commence Firing*

As Blondie and Tuco watch the Union and Confederate troops converge on the bridge, Blondie comments, "I've never seen so many men wasted so badly." As mentioned in chapter 3, this antiwar sentiment is significant because it not only reflects part of the character's personality, but is also a comment on war itself. As the battle continues, Tuco tells Blondie that the gold coins are buried on the other side of the river, and they decide to find explosives and destroy the bridge.

"Short March without Hope"

During the battle, the captain is wounded, and Blondie and Tuco see him as he is carried to safety on a stretcher. "The Strong" is heard again, with slightly different instrumentation, to inform the audience of his impending death. Blondie hands the captain a bottle and tells him to "Take a slug of this, Captain. Keep your ears open." Soon afterward, Blondie and Tuco carry some explosives past the troops and toward the bridge. As they do so, the "Marcetta senza Speranza" or "Short March without Hope" is heard. Blondie and Tuco then prepare to destroy the bridge.[32] The melody is hummed by a male chorus accompanied by a small ensemble of piano and percussion. Realizing the severe danger they are facing, Tuco suggests that they each divulge their part of the secret and tells Blondie that the gold coins are buried at Sad Hill Cemetery. Blondie tells Tuco the name on the grave is Arch Stanton, and he lights the fuse that ignites the explosives and destroys the bridge. The captain hears the explosion as he dies and "The Strong" is heard one final time, with its original instrumentation featuring the trumpet, to signify the death of another soldier.

"The Death of a Soldier"

Soon afterward, the battle ends and Blondie and Tuco find themselves alone by the river. The cue "The Death of a Soldier" is heard as they somehow make their way across the river and arrive on the other side where numerous bodies of dead Confederate soldiers are seen scattered across the landscape. This cue begins with music from the "Short March without Hope" sung without words by a male chorus accompanied by a harmonica. As they continue walking, Tuco looks at his map again, but Blondie does not seem to notice. Blondie and Tuco arrive at a bombed-out church and Blondie sees a dying Confederate soldier inside. He enters the church and offers the soldier his cigar as the music segues to an instrumental version of "The Story of a Soldier" as part of the same cue. The soldier dies and Blondie places his coat over the soldier's body. He then picks up a poncho that is nearby. This poncho is the same one that Clint Eastwood's character wore in the previous two Sergio Leone Westerns, making it appear that this film is a prequel to the two other Dollar films.

Blondie then notices that Tuco is riding away on horseback. As the audience hears Blondie's Motive 1A and the wah-wah version of Motive 2A, Blondie fires a cannon that is in front of the church, knocking Tuco off of the horse. Blondie reloads and fires the cannon again, and Tuco, who is now on foot, falls to the ground, hitting his head on a gravestone. He soon realizes that he has arrived at Sad Hill Cemetery.

"The Ecstasy of Gold"

What follows is perhaps the most exquisite blending of sound and image ever produced. After the sound of a single orchestral chime on the downbeat, not unlike the sound of a Spanish mission bell of the American Southwest, the audience hears the four-note piano ostinato that Morricone used in "The Desert," this time in duple meter, to begin the cue "The Ecstasy of Gold" (figure 5.17).

Figure 5.17: "The Ecstasy of Gold," Four-Note Ostinato in A Minor
from *The Good, the Bad and the Ugly* by Ennio Morricone
© 1966, 1968 (Renewed) Edizioni Eureka (Italy)
Rights for the world outside Italy controlled by U.S. Music International, Inc.
Rights in the U.S.A. and Canada administered by EMI Unart Catalog Inc. (Publishing)
and Warner Bros. Publications Inc. (Print)
All Rights Reserved. Used by Permission.
WARNER BROS. PUBLICATIONS U.S. INC., Miami, FL 33014

An English horn begins playing this beautifully haunting minor-key melody in the fifth measure of the cue (figure 5.18).[33] Morricone is once again using a melody based on a minor hexatonic scale, but this time it is a scale based on A. As the theme begins, Tuco is seen throwing away his map, a dog barks, and Tuco begins searching for Arch Stanton's grave.

As the cue is heard, Tuco makes his way to the center of the cemetery, where a large circular bed of stones is located. As he begins frantically searching for Arch Stanton's grave, the orchestral chime sounds again and a shorter, seventeen-measure version of the melody is heard, featuring the beautiful soprano voice that Morricone used in "The Carriage of the Spirits" to give the gold its unmistakably feminine quality. As Tuco's pace increases, the image repeatedly changes from close-ups of his face to shots of him running against an increasingly blurry background to dizzying images of the background itself, as if seen from his point of view. As the pace of the visual image increases, Morricone's orchestration continues to intensify.

A more concise twelve-measure version of the theme is heard again with a full orchestra and chorus. This is followed with the theme performed as a canon, or round, with some instruments playing one measure later then others. Morricone uses the wah-wah version of Motive 2A as part of a short transition before presenting the theme again, this time in a sixteen-measure version with more brass than was previously heard. He also changes the rhythm to include a triplet figure, three notes in the time of two. Tuco's pace continues to quicken and the theme is heard again featuring the horns. After a short transition, the complete theme is heard once more with full orchestra, followed by an eight-measure coda based on the theme. Then, in a moment of synchronization that might suggest that the film was edited to fit Morricone's music, the theme comes to an abrupt halt as Tuco suddenly stops in front of Arch Stanton's grave. Tuco believes he has finally found the grave where two hundred thousand dollars in gold coins are buried.

Figure 5.18: "The Ecstasy of Gold," English Horn Solo
from *The Good, the Bad and the Ugly* by Ennio Morricone
© 1966, 1968 (Renewed) Edizioni Eureka (Italy)
Rights for the world outside Italy controlled by U.S. Music International, Inc.
Rights in the U.S.A. and Canada administered by EMI Unart Catalog Inc. (Publishing)
and Warner Bros. Publications Inc. (Print)
All Rights Reserved. Used by Permission.
WARNER BROS. PUBLICATIONS U.S. INC., Miami, FL 33014

Some authors, including Jeff Smith,[34] have speculated that the music for this scene was written before the filming of the scene, as Morricone had done for "The Story of a Soldier" and all of Leone's *Once Upon a Time in the West.* When asked if this was indeed the case, Morricone answered, "The finale in the cemetery, when Tuco was seen to run around it, was scored after the filming of that particular scene, at the completion of editing and montage."[35] Eli Wallach concurs that there was no music being played during the filming of this scene. Wallach humorously recalls Leone's direction during the filming of this scene, "He said 'run' and I ran."[36] One must conclude, therefore, that this skillful union of music and image is unquestionably the result of Morricone's ability capture the dramatic energy of a scene and transform it to sonic experience for the viewer with incredible precision in the synchronization.

Cumbow elaborates on the effectiveness of this precise synchronization of image and sound:

> In all cinema, one of the most remarkable examples of an eminently visible and audible montage is the "Ecstasy of Gold" sequence from *The Good, the Bad and the Ugly:* On the piano's rolling repetition of a four-note figure, Morricone builds a simple but rapturous reed theme that, carried by female voice and strings, accelerates in tempo with the speed of Leone's montage and his swish pans.[37]

What Cumbow is saying, in effect, is that the tempo and rhythm of Morricone's music for this cue, which Morricone confirms was written after filming and editing, so closely imitates the tempo and rhythm of Leone's visual montage that the music is heard as an audible manifestation of the visual image. Morricone is able to achieve, through changes in tempo, rhythm, orchestration, and dynamics, a gradual increase in musical energy that matches, very precisely, the gradual increase in physical and emotional energy that Tuco is seen to experience as he comes closer and closer to reaching his goal.

After the music stops, Tuco begins to dig, but his digging is interrupted when somebody throws a shovel at him. Blondie's Motive 1A and the wah-wah version of Motive 2A are heard and the audience knows that Blondie has found Tuco. Blondie tells Tuco at gunpoint to dig, but they are both interrupted when somebody throws another shovel toward the grave, and the audience hears a short chord progression: D minor, G major, and D minor. These are the same chords that accompany Motives 1A and 2A in the A section of "Main Title," a chord progression that can only exist in the Dorian mode and can best be described as a Dorian Plagal progression (i – IV – i).[38] These chords are played on what sounds like an electric organ but with a timbre strikingly similar to that of the bass ocarina, the instrument that Morricone uses for Angel Eyes' Motive 1A. It is surprising that Morricone chose not to use Motive 1A to signify Angel Eyes' arrival at the gravesite.

Angel Eyes now tells Blondie at gunpoint to dig along with Tuco. The truth about the gold coins is revealed when Blondie kicks open the casket that Tuco has now uncovered and all three protagonists see Arch Stanton's decomposed body inside. Blondie tells Tuco and Angel Eyes that if they want to know the true location of the gold coins, they'll have to earn it. He claims to write the name of the grave that actually contains the gold coins on a stone and places the stone in the center of the large circular bed of stones nearby. As all three men take up positions around the circle, Morricone will once again blend his music with the visual image for yet another climactic moment.

"The Ecstasy of Gold," like "The Trio" that follows, is different than most cues in this film because this music only occurs once. Morricone attaches added significance to these two cues by presenting this music only once and by doing so near the climactic ending of the film.

"The Trio"

One of the last and most exciting musical cues in the film begins with a slow introduction alternating between a solo flute (figure 5.19) and a four-note guitar ostinato. Morricone cleverly and gradually increases the tension of this musical cue from almost nothing to an absolute fever pitch, during which Leone delivers an equally dramatic visual montage.

Figure 5.19: "The Trio," Flute Solo
from *The Good, the Bad and the Ugly* by Ennio Morricone
© 1966, 1968 (Renewed) Edizioni Eureka (Italy)
Rights for the world outside Italy controlled by U.S. Music International, Inc.
Rights in the U.S.A. and Canada administered by EMI Unart Catalog Inc. (Publishing)
and Warner Bros. Publications Inc. (Print)
All Rights Reserved. Used by Permission.
WARNER BROS. PUBLICATIONS U.S. INC., Miami, FL 33014

After the opening flute solo, the acoustic guitar enters with a four-note ostinato (figure 5.20), similar to the piano ostinato in "The Desert," with string accompaniment in the key of D minor. Each appearance of the ostinato lasts for exactly three measures (except in measures thirty through thirty-two, when it lasts for two measures and three beats, a possible mistake). In this cue, the ostinato recurs at different pitches to reflect changes in harmony. The first note of each group of four is an appoggiatura and the following three notes are an arpeggio of each chord. The repeated use of the ostinato throughout the film adds greater continuity to the score as a whole.

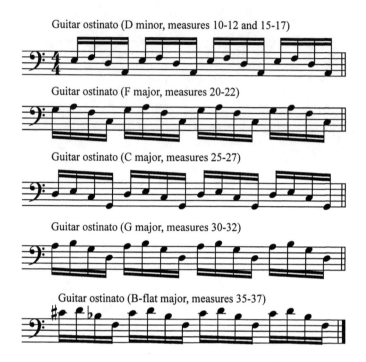

Figure 5.20: "The Trio," Guitar Ostinatos

from *The Good, the Bad and the Ugly* by Ennio Morricone
© 1966, 1968 (Renewed) Edizioni Eureka (Italy)
Rights for the world outside Italy controlled by U.S. Music International, Inc.
Rights in the U.S.A. and Canada administered by EMI Unart Catalog Inc. (Publishing)
and Warner Bros. Publications Inc. (Print)
All Rights Reserved. Used by Permission.
WARNER BROS. PUBLICATIONS U.S. INC., Miami, FL 33014

This introduction alternates between the guitar ostinatos, each one of which outlines a change in harmony, and the recurring flute solo that reinforces the D minor tonality each time. This dialogue between the two instruments creates harmonic tension as the scene begins to unfold. The suspense of the music and the visual image gradually increases until Morricone adds a full orchestra and chorus. There is a sudden crescendo in measures thirty-eight and thirty-nine before the main theme of this cue—a mariachi-style trumpet solo (figure 5.21)—begins in measure forty. As the theme begins, Leone changes from close-ups to a long shot, in preparation for the second crescendo in both the music and montage.

Figure 5.21: "The Trio," Trumpet Solo

This trumpet theme has a distinct southwestern flavor and is performed in an authentic mariachi style. Blondie, Tuco, and Angel Eyes have now reached their positions around the circle, forming a triangle. Morricone uses a mariachi-style trumpet solo just before or during the final confrontations between the pseudo-good and the evil of all three Dollar films. If one were to compare these three trumpet themes, it would become obvious that each one is more energetic than the one before. The solo featured in *The Good, the Bad and the Ugly* is the most intense and exciting of them all, ascending further into the brilliant high range of the instrument. It should be remembered that Morricone often reserves this majestic instrument for the most dramatic mo-

ments of a film, in this case "The Strong," "The Carriage of the Spirits," and "The Trio."

After the trumpet solo, there is a very abrupt halt in the musical
momentum that Miceli accurately and somewhat humorously describes
as "coitus interruptus."[39] The music stops and crows are heard in the
background. There is a short interlude before the theme returns. This
interlude, a different version of which appears on the soundtrack album, consists of timpani rolls, unusual percussion, bizarre electronic
sounds, the four-note piano ostinato from "The Desert," and musical
chimes (figure 5.22) that are unmistakably reminiscent of the pocket-
watch chimes that occur throughout *For a Few Dollars More.* The
three-note ostinatos in the chimes are derived from the four-note guitar
ostinatos in D minor and F major by combining the first two notes.

Figure 5.22: "The Trio," Chimes
from *The Good, the Bad and the Ugly* by Ennio Morricone
© 1966, 1968 (Renewed) Edizioni Eureka (Italy)
Rights for the world outside Italy controlled by U.S. Music International, Inc.
Rights in the U.S.A. and Canada administered by EMI Unart Catalog Inc. (Publishing)
and Warner Bros. Publications Inc. (Print)
All Rights Reserved. Used by Permission.
WARNER BROS. PUBLICATIONS U.S. INC., Miami, FL 33014

The original interlude, which appears on the soundtrack album, needed
to be changed to accommodate the final edit of the film. According to
Morricone, "After the recording, they wanted to modify the film's
montage, and, as the disk had already been recorded, I could change
only the music of the film's score itself. That music did not appear on
the disk."[40] Although the interlude that is heard in the film is vintage
Morricone, one should become familiar with the soundtrack album to
gain a glimpse of the composer's original intentions.

The theme is heard again, but this time, when the trumpet melody arrives at the A5 in the fifteenth measure (measure fifty-three of the original solo), the rhythm of the accompaniment changes to one resembling a Spanish bolero,[41] creating even more excitement and tension (the trumpet solo ends here in the film, but continues on the soundtrack album). Leone gives the audience a sense of the space between the three men by using a fast-moving montage of ever-increasing close-ups, until nothing but the men's eyes can be seen. The tension is finally released by the sound of a gunshot as Blondie shoots Angel Eyes. Blondie then fires three more times and the echo of the gunshots is deafening. As if choreographed like a ballet, one gunshot kills Angel Eyes and forces his collapsing body into an unused grave; a second shot places his hat in the grave; and a third shot does the same for his pistol. Brown summarizes:

> The entire scene, which lasts nearly five minutes (extremely long by standards of the American Western), represents a sophisticated instance of musically structured cinema via vertical montage, with Leone constructing a movement/retrograde-movement pattern in the visuals to complement Morricone's two crescendos, and via the dialectic established between the dynamic shot mixing and musical presence versus the static knee-shots and the absence of music.[42]

Brown is alluding to the fact that, unlike "The Ecstasy of Gold" in which music and image are united in a single crescendo from beginning to end, "The Trio" is actually one crescendo, followed by an abrupt halt, only to be concluded with a second crescendo. Brown seems to imply that Leone built this pattern around Morricone's music, but Morricone has made it clear that, with the exception of "The Story of a Soldier," his music for this film was written after the final edit of the montage was complete. Therefore, this cue was rewritten to accommodate the final edit of the montage.

It is soon revealed that this final contest to obtain the gold coins was not a fair fight. The cool, cunning, and manipulative Blondie had an unfair advantage, but Tuco, Angel Eyes, and the audience did not know it. Blondie had emptied Tuco's gun the previous night without Tuco's knowledge. Blondie knew that Angel Eyes posed the only real threat. Angel Eyes, however, was caught off guard as he divided his attention between Blondie and Tuco. Tuco, on the other hand, did not realize his vulnerability until after the danger had passed.

After the tension of this lengthy montage is finally released, Blondie forces Tuco at gunpoint to unearth the casket in the grave marked "Unknown" next to Arch Stanton's grave. They find the gold coins, but Blondie is not done manipulating his old friend and partner. Accompanied by the drumbeats from the introduction to the "Main Title," Blondie forces Tuco to put his neck in a noose and leaves him at the top of a grave marker to eventually fall and hang himself, or so the audience expects. Blondie ties Tuco's hands behind his back and rides off with half of the gold coins. However, so as not to disturb the equilibrium that exists between the two surviving protagonists, Blondie returns, and in one last gesture of goodness reminiscent of their earlier money-making scheme, cuts the rope from which Tuco is about to hang with a single gunshot and rides off. Tuco falls to the ground, the action freezes, and he receives his epithet "the ugly" on screen once more, accompanied by his Motive 1A. Angel Eyes' dead body is shown again as he is given named "the bad" and the audience hears his Motive 1A again. And the audience sees Blondie, who in turn is given the epithet "the good" once more as his Motive 1A is heard. As the drumbeats continue, Tuco gets up, runs toward Blondie and begins cursing him. Tuco's cursing ends humorously with his Motive 1A and the wah-wah version of Motive 2A. Blondie rides off into the distance and there is a reprise of music from the "Main Title," beginning with the B section, as the film ends.

Conclusions

Morricone's score for *The Good, the Bad and the Ugly* has withstood the test of time. What met with mediocre reviews from the American media when it was first heard in the 1960s has, over the years, been well-received and has met with critical acclaim, often being described as "operatic" in form, style, and function. The fact that so many different influences, many of which are often thought to be mutually exclusive, can be synthesized into one unmistakable compositional style is indeed the mark of a great craftsman. But Morricone is more than merely a craftsman. In this score, Morricone blends the influences of 1960s rock-and-roll, folk music, Italian popular music, Celtic and other ethnic music, Gregorian chant, serialism, musique concrète, Hollywood film scoring, and the avant-garde to create a logical and coherent opus.

Although Morricone follows many of the conventions of Hollywood film scoring in his music for *The Good, the Bad and the Ugly*, he contradicts many others. The most noticeable one is his use of minor keys for much of the fast and exciting music in this score, while using major keys for the sad and serious moments. Many of the Hollywood film composers of the period, following in the tradition of most classical composers, use major keys to depict excitement and minor keys to depict more serious moments.

Motives and Ostinatos

The consistency with which Morricone uses each protagonist's Motives 1A, 1B, 2A, 2B, 2C, and 2D is remarkable and obviously intentional. Blondie is always represented by the soprano recorder version of Motives 1A and 1B, after which Motives 2A, 2B, 2C, or 2D, if they occur, are always heard with the unusual wah-wah sound, that metallic-sounding male voice. Tuco is always represented by the coyote version of Motives 1A and 1B, after which Motives 2A, 2B, 2C, or 2D, if they occur, are also heard with the unusual wah-wah sound. Angel Eyes' Motives 1A and 1B are always heard on the bass ocarina; however, they are not always followed by the same version of Motives 2A, 2B, 2C, and 2D. Twice, Angel Eyes' Motive 1A is followed by Motive 2A on the electric guitar. In the "Main Title," his Motives 1A and 1B are followed by Motives 2A, 2B, 2C, and 2D as a human whistle. There is also a reprise of music from the A section of the "Main Title" in which his Motives 1A and 1B are followed by the other motives played on the flute. Angel Eyes' Motives 1A and 1B are never followed by the wah-wah version of Motives 2A, 2B, 2C, or 2D, because its humorous and flippant quality would certainly seem inappropriate for a character so completely sinister.

Each of the three protagonists is given his respective version of Motive 1A during a freeze-frame in which his epithet appears on the screen. For no clear reason, the epithets first appear in red. During the film's final scene, the three are given their epithets once more, but in different colors. After Tuco falls from the top of the grave marker, his epithet appears in green. Angel Eyes' dead body is shown as his appears in red, and Blondie's then appears in yellow.

The fact that Motive 1A of the "Main Title" has become so easily recognized by the moviegoing public and has been given extramusical meaning in other films and other media is not only remarkable in itself, but is a testament to Morricone's ability to create themes that are easily remembered by the audience. Music from the "Main Title" has been used in other films, including *Every Which Way but Loose* (1978), starring Clint Eastwood, Disney's *The Lion King $1^1/_2$* (2004), and several television commercials, typically as a signifier of things American, Western, masculine, confrontational, or a combination of two or more of these concepts.

Morricone cleverly uses similar, and occasionally identical, four-note ostinatos in several cues. The four-note ostinato first heard in "The Rope Bridge" reappears later in "The Desert," "The Ecstasy of Gold," and "The Trio." The repetition of this minimalist device gives the score a greater sense of continuity, while Morricone is able to create a great deal of variety at the same time.

Key Relationships

Key relationships occupy a small space in the architecture of an Ennio Morricone score. Unlike his Hollywood counterparts, who use numerous keys to represent different characters or different abstract concepts, Morricone chooses only a few different keys for this score. Much of the score is in D minor or D Dorian, such as the "Main Title," "The Sundown," and "The Trio." D minor is the same key Morricone chose for much of the music in *A Fistful of Dollars* and *For a Few Dollars More*, including the "Main Title" and the mariachi trumpet solo in each film. Throughout history, the key of D minor has been used by composers for many of their most serious works, including Johann Sebastian Bach's *Toccata and Fugue in D Minor*, Wolfgang Amadeus Mozart's *Piano Concerto No. 20* (K. 466) and *Requiem* (K. 626), and Beethoven's *Ninth Symphony*.

The parallel major of D minor, D major, is used for the "Short March," "Short March without Hope," the very serious and somber "The Story of a Soldier," and "The Death of a Soldier." Morricone also chose D major for the "Main Title" of Sergio Leone's *Once Upon a Time in the West*, not D minor as he did for the first three Westerns of Leone.

"The Desert" appears to be in A minor, as suggested by the repeated ostinatos, but the tonality of that cue is intentionally vague. A minor is also the key of "The Ecstasy of Gold." B-flat major is reserved for the military bugle calls as well as "The Strong" and "The Carriage of the Spirits," which include bugle calls played ad libitum.

Diegetic Music

There are only a few instances of diegetic music in this film. The first is the horse-drawn wagon of men singing as they throw Maria, Bill Carson's girlfriend, from the wagon. The second instance is the "Short March," but the source of that music is ambiguous. The audience is led to believe that the harmonica and whistling are diegetic, but nobody is seen playing the harmonica or whistling.

Other instances of diegetic music are the military bugle calls that are heard when Blondie and Tuco are at the prison camp, and again when they are at the Union Army camp at the bridge. As mentioned in chapter 2, these calls appear to be diegetic, but no bugler is ever seen by the audience.

The historical accuracy with which these bugle calls have been selected for their place in the film's narrative demonstrates a keen desire for what was a new kind of realism in the Western genre at the time. This realism is evident, not only in the authentic use of these bugle calls, but in many of the visual details of the film as well. Although it is well known that director Sergio Leone strived for as much visual realism as possible in this film, even using authentic Civil War artillery, Morricone is quick to point out that the composer is the one who must make any musical decision. When asked about these bugle calls, Morricone seemed uncertain as to their selection for the film, but it was most likely he who decided what bugle calls were to be used in this film and when.[43]

One other instance of diegetic music is the song "The Story of a Soldier," which is sung by prisoners at the Union Army camp where Blondie and Tuco are detained. This song is later sung at a time and place—as Tuco kills Wallace after jumping off the train—when the audience knows that no characters in the film are singing.

A Palette of Many Colors

Much has already been written about Morricone's unconventional orchestrations in *The Good, the Bad and the Ugly* and the other Leone Westerns. Unlike his Hollywood contemporaries, Morricone does not limit himself to the typical studio orchestra of strings, woodwinds, brass, and the standard symphonic percussion instruments. His use of bells, orchestral chimes, the soprano recorder, the bass ocarina, the human voice, the human whistle, acoustic guitar, electric guitar, electric organ, piano, and harmonica make this colorful score unmistakably the work of Morricone.

Figuratively speaking, Morricone is a painter whose palette includes many colors. He does not hesitate to use any of these colors, in any combination, if it will enable him to reach his desired goal. He paints a musical picture that informs and occasionally surprises his audience. Since the Westerns of the 1960s and 1970s, he has continued to expand his palette to include more modern instruments, such as the soprano saxophone and flugelhorn that he used in *Malèna* to highlight the dissimilarity between the young man and the mature woman, as well as instruments from the past, such as the harpsichord and oboe that he used in *The Mission* to represent the western European missionaries in seventeenth-century South America. It is likewise refreshing that his musical palette, which includes some electric instruments, has not become diluted with numerous electronically synthesized sounds, but is rich with the sounds of acoustic instruments and human voices.

Ennio Morricone

Evidently, there are numerous stylistic factors that contribute to the fact that a score such as *The Good, the Bad and the Ugly* has a sound that is unquestionably "Morriconian." These include all musical elements: melody, harmony, rhythm, form, timbre, and dynamics. One might think that such a compositional style could be easily imitated, but in the hands of another composer, these same contributing factors would almost certainly yield lesser results. Morricone's compositional style is more than merely the sum of its parts. It is also the result of a work ethic typically found only in composers of concert music, combined with an unquenchable desire for experimentation.

After his collaborations with Sergio Leone, Morricone went on to score numerous other films. His style has continued to evolve, never truly staying the same but always unmistakably that of Morricone, reflecting an eclectic and ever-expanding blend of musical genres, and yet always accessible to the average moviegoer.

Perhaps Morricone's most significant contribution to the art of film music is not found in a single film score; rather, it is his passionate desire to continue to experiment and innovate for the sake of innovation itself and not solely for the sake of creating film music that is artistically and commercially successful.

Morricone maintains a demanding schedule of composing, orchestrating, conducting, and recording, being constantly motivated by his rare and admirable work ethic. His name almost always appears after the words "music composed, orchestrated, and conducted by" in the credits of the films for which he has written music. He diligently maintains his practice of orchestrating and conducting all of the film scores that he composes, insisting that only the composer should put the finishing touches on the music. In spite of this commendable methodology, he does not believe that his work is any harder than it should be. As he told Kennedy in 1991, "I don't believe that I do work hard. I don't believe that I work too much. Think of J. S. Bach; think of W. Mozart and of many others. Their music was their life. Without being as great as they, the same is true for me. I'm not tired of writing music. It's the only thing that I believe I know how to do."[44] It may indeed be the only thing he believes he knows how to do, but he does it very well, a fact for which all who enjoy his numerous contributions to film music should be grateful.

APPENDIX

SELECTED FILMOGRAPHY OF ENNIO MORRICONE

The following is a chronological listing of many of Ennio Morricone's most representative film scores. Most titles appear in English as they did for the films' American release. The dates included here are the release dates of the films in the United States. Many of these films, especially the earlier ones, had been released in Italy at least one year earlier.

1965   *Il federale (The Facist)*, directed by Luciano Salce, starring Ugo Tagnazzi and Georges Wilson

1967   *The Battle of Algiers*, directed by Gillo Pontecorvo, starring Brahim Haggiag and Jean Martin (additional music by Gillo Pontecorvo)

1967   *A Fistful of Dollars* (as Dan Savio), directed by Sergio Leone, starring Clint Eastwood and Gian Maria Volonté

1967   *For a Few Dollars More*, directed by Sergio Leone, starring Clint Eastwood, Gian Maria Volonté, and Lee Van Cleef

1967   *The Good, the Bad and the Ugly*, directed by Sergio Leone, starring Clint Eastwood, Lee Van Cleef, and Eli Wallach

1969   *Once Upon a Time in the West*, directed by Sergio Leone, starring Henry Fonda, Claudia Cardinale, Jason Robards, and Charles Bronson

1970   *Two Mules for Sister Sara*, directed by Don Siegel, starring
        Clint Eastwood and Shirley MacLaine

1972   *A Fistful of Dynamite* (a.k.a. *Duck, You Sucker*), directed by
        Sergio Leone, starring James Coburn and Rod Steiger

1973   *My Name Is Nobody*, directed by Tonino Valerii and Sergio
        Leone, starring Henry Fonda and Terence Hill

1977   *Exorcist II: The Heretic*, directed by John Boorman, starring
        Linda Blair and Richard Burton

1977   *Orca*, directed by Michael Anderson, starring Richard Harris
        and Charlotte Rampling

1978   *Days of Heaven* (Academy Award Nomination for Morri-
        cone), directed by Terrence Malick, starring Richard Gere and
        Brooke Adams

1979   *Bloodline*, directed by Terence Young, starring Audrey Hep-
        burn, Ben Gazzara, and James Mason

1982   *The Thing*, directed by John Carpenter, starring Kurt Russell
        and Wilford Brimley

1984   *Once Upon a Time in America*, directed by Sergio Leone, star-
        ring Robert De Niro and James Woods

1986   *The Mission* (Academy Award Nomination for Morricone),
        directed by Roland Joffé, starring Robert De Niro and Jeremy
        Irons

1987   *The Untouchables* (Academy Award Nomination for Morri-
        cone), directed by Brian De Palma, starring Kevin Costner,
        Sean Connery, Andy Garcia, and Robert De Niro

1989   *Cinema Paradiso*, directed by Giuseppe Tornatore, starring
        Philippe Noiret, Jacques Perrin, and Salvatore Cascio

1989   *Casualties of War*, directed by Brian De Palma, starring Mi-
        chael J. Fox and Sean Penn

1990   *Hamlet*, directed by Franco Zeffirelli, starring Mel Gibson and
        Glenn Close

1991   *Bugsy* (Academy Award Nomination for Morricone), directed
        by Barry Levinson, starring Warren Beatty and Annette
        Bening

1993   *In the Line of Fire*, directed by Wolfgang Petersen, starring
        Clint Eastwood, John Malkovich, and Rene Russo

1994   *Disclosure*, directed by Barry Levinson, starring Michael
        Douglas, Demi Moore, and Donald Sutherland

1998   *Bulworth*, directed by Warren Beatty, starring Warren Beatty

1998   *The Legend of 1900*, directed by Giuseppe Tornatore, starring Tim Roth

2000   *Mission to Mars*, directed by Brian De Palma, starring Gary Sinise and Tim Robbins

2000   *Malèna* (Academy Award Nomination for Morricone), directed by Giuseppe Tornatore, starring Monica Bellucci and Giuseppe Sulfaro

NOTES

Chapter 1

1. Jay Cocks, "The Lyrical Assassin at 5 A.M." *Time*, 16 March 1987, 83.

2. Cocks, 83.

3. Sergio Miceli, *Morricone: la musica, il cinema* (Modena, Italy: Mucchi Editore, 1994), 15-17.

4. Miceli, *Morricone: la musica, il cinema*, 17.

5. Adam Sweeting, "Mozart of Film Music." *The Guardian* (Manchester), 23 February 2001.

6. Jeff Smith, *The Sounds of Commerce: Marketing Popular Film Music* (New York: Columbia University Press, 1998), 133.

7. Laurence E. MacDonald, *The Invisible Art of Film Music: A Comprehensive History* (New York: Ardsley House, Publishers, Inc., 1998), 310–11.

8. Ennio Morricone, fax sent to the author, translated by Albert Balesh, M.D., 26 March 2004.

9. Christopher Frayling, *Spaghetti Westerns: Cowboys and Europeans from Karl May to Sergio Leone* (New York: I. B. Tauris & Co. Ltd., 1998), 147.

10. Frayling, 165.

11. Royal S. Brown, *Overtones and Undertones: Reading Film Music* (Berkeley: University of California Press, 1994), 232.

12. Sweeting, no page.

13. Sergio Miceli, "Ennio Morricone," in *The New Grove Dictionary of Music and Musicians*, 2nd ed., vol. 17, edited by Stanley Sadie (London: Macmillan Publishers Limited, 2001), 145.

14. Miceli, "Ennio Morricone," 146.

15. Joe Gore, "The Good, the Great, and the Godly: Ennio Morricone's Miraculous Soundscapes," translated by Giorgio Saluti, *Guitar Player*, April 1997, 59.

16. Ennio Morricone, interview with author, translated by Albert Balesh, M.D., Rome, 26 July 2003.

Chapter 2

1. Jon Burlingame and Gary Crowdus, "Music at the Service of the Cinema: An Interview with Ennio Morricone," translated by Lena Erin and Vivian Treves, *Cineaste* 21, nos. 1–2 (1995): 77.

2. Ennio Morricone, interview with author.

3. MacDonald, 310.

4. Randall D. Larson, *Musique Fantastique: A Survey of Film Music in the Fantastic Cinema* (Metuchen, N.J.: The Scarecrow Press, Inc., 1985), 196.

5. MacDonald, 310.

6. Robert C. Cumbow, *Once Upon a Time: The Films of Sergio Leone* (Metuchen, N.J.: The Scarecrow Press Inc., 1987), 204.

7. Harlan Kennedy, "The Harmonious Background," *American Film* 16, no. 2 (February 1991): 41.

8. Cumbow, 200–201.

9. Burlingame and Crowdus, 76.

10. Jeff Smith, 134.

11. Philip Tagg, "The Virginian: Life, Liberty and the US Pursuit of Happiness," 368 (unpublished).

12. Cumbow, 204.

13. Larson, 327.

14. Gore, 57.

15. Burlingame and Crowdus, 77.

16. Jeff Smith, 20.

17. Russell Lack, *Twenty Four Frames Under: A Buried History of Film Music* (London: Quartet Books, 1997), 190–91.

18. Gary Marmorstein, *Hollywood Rhapsody: Movie Music and Its Makers, 1900 to 1975* (New York: Schirmer Books, 1997), 303–304.

19. MacDonald, 211.

20. Jeff Smith, 153.

21. Jeff Smith, 153.

22. Ennio Morricone, interview with author.

23. For a more detailed musical example of this figure, see Miceli, *Morricone: la musica, il cinema*, 110.

24. Miceli, *Morricone: la musica, il cinema*, translated by author, 113.

25. For a more detailed musical example of this figure, see Miceli, *Morricone: la musica, il cinema*, 125.

26. Ennio Morricone, interview with author.

27. Ennio Morricone, interview with author. When asked about his use of minor keys in Westerns, Morricone played a D Dorian scale on the piano, followed by the A section of the "Main Title" from *The Good, the Bad and the Ugly*. Although it appears to be in D minor, the melody consists of the six notes of the D minor hexatonic scale. However, the repeated occurrence of B-naturals in the harmonization suggests the Dorian mode. B-natural also appears in the melody of the B section of the "Main Title."

28. Cumbow, 202.

29. See Miceli, *Morricone: la musica, il cinema*, 118.

30. The B-flat trumpet is a transposing instrument that sounds a major second lower than written. Music examples contained herein are notated at sounding pitch and not at the B-flat trumpet's written pitch.

31. See Miceli, *Morricone: la musica, il cinema*, 125.

32. Burlingame and Crowdus, 77.

Chapter 3

1. *Per un Pugno di Dollari* literally translates as *For a Handful of Dollars*.

2. Jeff Smith, 135.

3. Edward Gallafent, *Clint Eastwood: Actor and Director* (London: Studio Vista, 1994), 26.

4. Renata Adler, "The Burn, the Gouge, and the Mangle." *New York Times*, 25 January 1968, 33.

5. Brian Garfield, *Western Films: A Complete Guide* (New York: Rawson Associates, 1982), 178.

6. Pat H. Broeske, *Magill's Survey of Cinema: Foreign Language Films*, vol. 3, edited by Frank N. Magill. (Englewood Cliffs, N.J.: Salem Press, 1985), 1256.

7. Paul Smith, *Clint Eastwood: A Cultural Production* (Minneapolis: University of Minnesota Press, 1993), 1.

8. John H. Lenihan, *Showdown: Confronting Modern America in the Western Film* (Urbana: University of Illinois Press, 1980), 47.

9. Lenihan, 53.

10. Eli Wallach, telephone conversation with author, 17 October 2003.

11. Dennis Bingham, *Acting Male: Masculinities in the Films of James Stewart, Jack Nicholson, and Clint Eastwood* (New Brunswick, N.J.: Rutgers University Press, 1994), 169.

12. *The Good, the Bad and the Ugly*, dir. Sergio Leone, 161 min. MGM Home Entertainment, 1998, Digital Video Disk.

13. "From Cowboy to Composer: Clint Eastwood Takes the Reins on Hollywood and Makes His Mark in Music." *International Musician*, October 2003, 17.

14. Mr. Wallach has requested that his date of birth not be included here. Eli Wallach, telephone conversation with author.

15. Eli Wallach, telephone conversation with author.

16. In many reliable sources, including *The American Film Institute Catalog*, *Magill's Survey of Cinema*, and the *New York Times* review, this character's name is spelled "Setenza." However, in other sources, including the Italian DVD and the Compact Disc from GDM, his name is spelled "Sentenza." In my opinion, the correct spelling is "Setenza."

17. Eli Wallach, telephone conversation with author.

18. Paul Smith, 9.

19. Marcia Landy, "He Went Thataway: The Form and Style of Leone's Italian Westerns," in *The Western Reader*, ed. Jim Kitses and Gregg Rickman (New York: Limelight Editions, 1998), 218.

20. Cumbow, 47-48.

21. *The Good, the Bad and the Ugly*, Digital Video Disk.

Chapter 4

1. Sergio Miceli and Ennio Morricone, *Comporre per il Cinema*, translated by author (Venice: Fondazione Scuola Nazionale di Cinema, 2001), 165.

2. Bosley Crowther, "A Fistful of Dollars." *New York Times*, 2 February 1967, 29.

3. Bosley Crowther, "For a Few Dollars More." *New York Times*, 4 July 1967, 23.

4. "Western Grand Guignol." *Time*, 21 July 1967, 76.

5. Joseph Morgenstern, "The Via Veneto Kid." *Newsweek*, 24 July 1967, 76.

6. Cumbow, 207.

7. "The Good, the Bad and the Ugly." *Variety*, 27 December 1967, 6.

8. *The Rolling Stone Record Guide* (New York: Random House, Inc., 1979), 564.

9. Garfield, 178.

10. Sweeting, no page.

11. Tagg, 370.

12. Burlingame and Crowdus, 80.

Chapter 5

1. The film's cue sheet, which presumably lists the musical cues as they appeared in the film's original Italian theatrical release, does not list titles for the cues, only numbers. Unfortunately, the cue numbers and running times on the cue sheet are illegible.

2. Miceli, *Morricone: la musica, il cinema*, 134.

3. Miceli, *Morricone: la musica, il cinema*, 134.

4. Ennio Morricone, interview with author.

5. Miceli, *Morricone: la musica, il cinema*, 134.

6. This exposition of the three versions of Motive 1A is not included in the film's commercially available soundtrack recording Compact Disc.

7. For a more detailed musical example of this figure, see Miceli, *Morricone: la musica, il cinema*, 132.

8. Ennio Morricone, interview with author. When asked what instruments were used for this sound, Morricone simply sang the motive while moving his hand over his mouth to create the wah-wah effect.

9. Miceli, *Morricone: la musica, il cinema*, 134.

10. The sounds of gunshots heard during the "Main Title," like many of the sound effects that occur during music in this film, are not included on the soundtrack album.

11. Ennio Morricone, interview with author.

12. Tagg, 304.

13. In some English-language prints of the film, these epithets appear in their original Italian. On the DVD released in the United States, they appear in English.

14. Jeff Smith, 149.

15. The guitar is a transposing instrument that sounds one octave lower than written. Music examples contained herein are notated at sounding pitch and not at the guitar's written pitch.

16. The next scene, which was deleted from the original English-language version and restored in 2003, shows Tuco with a chicken as he arrives at a campsite. He is looking for his three friends, Pedro, Chico, and Ramón, who are brothers. He finds them and offers to pay each of them one thousand dollars if they help him find Blondie, who has taken all of the reward money from their previous capers. These are the three men who are later seen attempting to surprise Blondie at a hotel while he is cleaning his gun.

This scene includes a short musical cue that includes a beautiful eight-measure flute, oboe, and English horn melody in D major and ends with Motive 1A played on the English horn and Motive 2A featuring the wah-wah sound. This music is also heard as part of the cue "Mission San Antonio" (figure 5.9). This music does not appear on the original soundtrack album released by United Artists Records, but it is included in the cue "Mission San Antonio" on the complete soundtrack recording released by GDM.

This scene was included in the *American Movie Classics* broadcast on 10 May 2003, but this is the only deleted scene that is not included as a bonus track, in Italian, on the Digital Video Disk (DVD) that was released in the United States. Likewise, this scene does not appear as part of the feature film on the Italian DVD.

17. In the Italian version of the film, a scene occurs here in which Angel Eyes arrives at a bombed-out Confederate camp looking for Bill Carson. As he dismounts and looks around, the cue "The Strong" (fig-

ure 5.8) is heard for the first time. In addition to this beautiful solo trumpet melody, military bugle calls are performed ad libitum. This is why the cues appear to be out of order on the soundtrack album. If this scene had been included in the original English-language version, the soundtrack album cues would be in the correct order.

Angel Eyes finds many wounded soldiers inside the camp. He talks to one of the Confederate soldiers and inquires about Bill Carson. The soldier does not answer the question until Angel Eyes gives him a bottle of red wine. Angel Eyes finds out that Bill Carson is with the Third Cavalry, that they have left, and that he is probably dead.

This scene, and all of the deleted scenes that follow, are included as bonus tracks on the American DVD in Italian and on the restored version of the film that was broadcast by *American Movie Classics* in English. Since Lee Van Cleef passed away before the restoration was made, another actor's voice is heard as the voice of Angel Eyes.

18. The English horn is a transposing instrument that sounds a perfect fifth lower than written. Music examples contained herein are notated at sounding pitch and not at the English horn's written pitch.

19. Jeff Smith, 140.

20. This scene is longer in the Italian version of the film. The deleted footage is included in the restored English-language version, as a bonus track on the American DVD, and in the Italian DVD version of the film.

21. Jeff Smith, 139.

22. In the Italian version of the film, a scene occurs here in which Tuco and Blondie arrive at a Confederate camp at night. Tuco is looking for medical help for Blondie. He finds none, but learns that they are in Apache Canyon, New Mexico, and that Mission San Antonio, where he can get help, is nearby. The audience soon learns that Tuco's brother, Pablo, is a priest at the mission. This scene includes no music.

23. The deleted scene that occurs here in the Italian version of the film shows Blondie and Tuco traveling in the stagecoach. Tuco is carefully studying a map so they can make their way to Sad Hill Cemetery. Tuco is seen studying this map on several occasions later in the film. The appearance of the map later in the film in the American DVD version is unexpected, since the first appearances of the map were deleted.

This scene includes a short version of the cue "The Carriage of the Spirits" as Blondie and Tuco discuss the dead soldiers they see along the road.

24. This cue is slightly longer in the film than on the original soundtrack album. The lyrics included here are those in the film. The original soundtrack album includes the first half of verse one (measures one through eight), the second half of verse two (measures nine through seventeen), and all of verse three. According to some sources, the lyrics for the last phrase of the first verse should be "and smile as you say goodbye," but in the film, it is clear that the lyrics "and smile as you go" are being sung. All four verses that are heard in the film appear on the complete soundtrack album released by GDM.

25. On the Italian DVD, this interlude is slightly different. Also, in the Italian version, the verses appear in a slightly different order. After verses one and two, the first half of verse three is hummed. After verse three, the first half of verse one is heard again followed by the second half of verse two. The interlude is next, hummed rather than played. This is followed by verse four, but measures seven through nine are omitted, most likely for timing.

26. Brown, 228.

27. Ennio Morricone, interview with author.

28. Eli Wallach, telephone conversation with author. Due to the fact that this cue is slightly different in the Italian version of the film, which was made before the film was dubbed in English, it is logical to assume that it was the cue as it appears in the Italian version that was being played during the filming of this scene.

29. In the Italian version of the film, a scene occurs here in which Blondie is seen camping out with Angel Eyes. As the other members of Angel Eyes' gang arrive at the campsite, Blondie shoots and kills one of them. There is no music in this scene.

30. The sudden appearance of Tuco's map seems unusual. The first appearance of the map is in a scene that was deleted from the original English-language prints.

31. The deleted scene that occurs here in the Italian version shows Blondie, Tuco, and the captain talking about the battle. The captain continues drinking as he asks them their names, but no answers are given. The next music cue, the "Short March" played slowly on the harmonica, begins during the deleted footage.

32. This scene is slightly longer in the Italian version.

33. For a more detailed musical example of this figure, see Miceli, *Morricone: la musica, il cinema*, 137.

34. Jeff Smith, 151.

35. Ennio Morricone, interview with author.

36. Eli Wallach, telephone conversation with author.

37. Cumbow, 201.

38. A plagal cadence, IV – I in a major key or less often iv – i in a minor key, is also called the "Amen" cadence because it appears at the end of many Christian hymns. Typically, both chords are either major or minor. Only in the Dorian mode will the tonic triad (i) be minor and the subdominant triad (IV) be major.

39. Miceli, *Morricone: la musica, il cinema*, 135.

40. Ennio Morricone, interview with author.

41. A traditional Spanish bolero is actually in triple meter, not a quadruple meter as in this example.

42. Brown, 229.

43. Ennio Morricone, interview with author.

44. Kennedy, 46.

BIBLIOGRAPHY

Adler, Renata. "The Burn, the Gouge, and the Mangle." *New York Times*, 25 January 1968, 33.

Bingham, Dennis. *Acting Male: Masculinities in the Films of James Stewart, Jack Nicholson, and Clint Eastwood*. New Brunswick, N.J.: Rutgers University Press, 1994.

Broeske, Pat H. *Magill's Survey of Cinema: Foreign Language Films*, edited by Frank N. Magill, vol. 3, 1252–57. Englewood Cliffs, N.J.: Salem Press, 1985.

Brown, Jeremy K. "Ennio Morricone." *Current Biography* 61, no. 10 (2000): 64–67.

Brown, Royal S. *Overtones and Undertones: Reading Film Music*. Berkeley: University of California Press, 1994.

Il buono, il brutto, il cattivo. Directed by Sergio Leone. 168 min. Cine Video Corporation, no date, DVD.

Burlingame, Jon. *Sound and Vision: Sixty Years of Motion Picture Soundtracks*. New York: Billboard Books, 2000.

Burlingame, Jon and Gary Crowdus. "Music at the Service of the Cinema: An Interview with Ennio Morricone." Translated by Lena Erin and Vivian Treves. *Cineaste* 21, nos. 1–2 (1995): 76–80.

Canty, Captain Daniel J. *Bugle Signals, Calls & Marches*. Bryn Mawr, Pa.: Oliver Ditson Company, 1916.

Cocks, Jay. "The Lyrical Assassin at 5 A.M." *Time*, 16 March 1987, 83.

Crowther, Bosley. "A Fistful of Dollars." *New York Times*, 2 February 1967, 29.

————. "For a Few Dollars More." *New York Times*, 4 July 1967, 23.

Cumbow, Robert C. *Once Upon a Time: The Films of Sergio Leone*. Metuchen, N.J.: The Scarecrow Press Inc., 1987.

Darby, William and Jack Du Bios. *American Film Music: Major Com-
    posers, Techniques, Trends, 1915–1990*. Jefferson, N.C.: McFar-
    land & Company, Inc., 1990.
Frayling, Christopher. *Spaghetti Westerns: Cowboys and Europeans
    from Karl May to Sergio Leone*. New York: I. B. Tauris & Co.
    Ltd., 1998.
"From Cowboy to Composer: Clint Eastwood Takes the Reins in Hol-
    lywood and Makes His Mark in Music." *International Musician*,
    October 2003, 16-17.
Gallafent, Edward. *Clint Eastwood: Actor and Director*. London: Stu-
    dio Vista, 1994.
Garfield, Brian. *Western Films: A Complete Guide*. New York: Rawson
    Associates, 1982.
The Good, the Bad and the Ugly. Directed by Sergio Leone. 161 min.
    MGM Home Entertainment, 1998, DVD.
"The Good, the Bad and the Ugly." *Variety*, 27 December 1967, 6.
Gore, Joe. "The Good, the Great, and the Godly: Ennio Morricone's
    Miraculous Soundscapes." Translated by Giorgio Saluti. *Guitar
    Player* 31, April 1997, 57–60.
Jacobson, Mark. "Symphony for a Hanging." *Esquire*, October 1995,
    170.
Karlin, Fred. *Listening to Movies: The Film Lover's Guide to Film Mu-
    sic*. New York: Schirmer Books, 1994.
Kennedy, Harlan. "The Harmonious Background." *American Film* 16,
    no. 2 (February 1991): 39–41, 46.
Krafsur, Richard P., ed. *The American Film Institute Catalog of Motion
    Pictures*, vol. F6. New York: R. R. Bowker Company, 1976.
Lack, Russell. *Twenty Four Frames Under: A Buried History of Film
    Music*. London: Quartet Books, 1997.
Landy, Marcia. "He Went Thataway: The Form and Style of Leone's
    Italian Westerns." In *The Western Reader*, edited by Jim Kitses
    and Gregg Rickman. New York: Limelight Editions, 1998.
Larson, Randall D. *Musique Fantastique: A Survey of Film Music in
    the Fantastic Cinema*. Metuchen, N.J.: The Scarecrow Press, Inc.,
    1985.
Lenihan, John H. *Showdown: Confronting Modern America in the
    Western Film*. Urbana: University of Chicago Press, 1980.
Lhassa, Anne and Jean Lhassa. *Ennio Morricone: Biographie*.
    Lausanne, Switzerland: Editions Favre S.A., 1989.

MacDonald, Laurence E. *The Invisible Art of Film Music: A Comprehensive History*. New York: Ardsley House Publishers, Inc., 1998.

Marmorstein, Gary. *Hollywood Rhapsody: Movie Music and Its Makers, 1900 to 1975*. New York: Schirmer Books, 1997.

Marsh, Dave and John Swenson. *The Rolling Stone Record Guide*. New York: Random House, Inc., 1979.

Miceli, Sergio. "Ennio Morricone." In *The New Grove Dictionary of Music and Musicians*, 2nd ed., edited by Stanley Sadie, vol. 17, 145–46. London: Macmillan Publishers Limited, 2001.

————. *Morricone: la musica, il cinema*. Modena, Italy: Mucchi Editore, 1994.

Morgenstern, Joseph. "The Via Veneto Kid." *Newsweek*, 24 July 1967, 76.

Morricone, Ennio. *The Good, the Bad and the Ugly: Original Motion Picture Soundtrack*. EMI-Manhattan Records CDP 7 48408 2, CD.

Morricone, Ennio and Sergio Miceli. *Comporre per il cinema*. Venice: Fondazione Scuola Nazionale di Cinema, 2001.

Restagno, Enzo. "Goffredo Petrassi." In *The New Grove Dictionary of Music and Musicians*, 2nd ed., edited by Stanley Sadie, vol. 19, 499-503. London: Macmillan Publishers Limited, 2001.

Schmidt, Elaine. "Morricone: Music." *American Record Guide* 62, no. 6 (1999): 177.

Smith, Jeff. *The Sounds of Commerce: Marketing Popular Film Music*. New York: Columbia University Press, 1998.

Smith, Paul. *Clint Eastwood: A Cultural Production*. Minneapolis: University of Minnesota Press, 1993.

Sweeting, Adam. "Mozart of Film Music." *The Guardian*, Manchester, 23 February 2001.

Tagg, Philip. "The Virginian: Life, Liberty and the US Pursuit of Happiness" (unpublished).

"Western Grand Guignol." *Time*, 21 July 1967, 76.

INDEX

ABOUT THE AUTHOR

Charles Leinberger is a Professor of Music at the University of Texas at El Paso (U.S.A.). He has a Bachelor of Music degree from Northern Arizona University, a Master of Music degree from the University of Miami, and a Doctor of Philosophy degree from the University of Arizona.